Fishing
with my father

OTHER BOOKS BY THE SAME AUTHOR

The Puffin Book of Freshwater Fishing

Fishing
with my father

Roger Pierce

Published in 1993 by
The Chiltern Agency
Kingston Stert
Chinnor
Oxford OX9 4NL

British Library Cataloguing in Publication Data

A catalogue record for this book is available from the British Library.

ISBN 0–9521618–0–X

Designed and produced by Images Design and Print Ltd
Printed and bound in Great Britain by Hartnolls Ltd, Bodmin, Cornwall

South-west Scotland: late June 1992. As my son Matthew and I left the cottage at 10 p.m. the light was only just beginning to fade. At this time of year and in this part of the world the darkness which so much increases the chance of a sea-trout lasts not much more than three hours. Even at one in the morning it's still not pitch black. With plenty of time to spare we sat on the wall in front of the cottage to check the gear. Each carried two 10' 6" rods, one with a floating line and one with a sinker. Landing nets hung on webbing slings, and the bare essentials of fly wallet, spool of nylon, sharpening stone, torch and priest went into the front pocket of our chest waders. Night fly-fishing is hard enough work without being weighed down by superfluous kit. The fishing bags containing coffee and spare tackle would be left at one of the fishing huts.

The little river was looking its best. Upstream was a handsome stone bridge. On it, as usual, a few figures had succumbed to the endless fascination of bridge-leaning. The previous year there had been scenes of great excitement as two unexpected grilse were spotted, but this time all was calm. If anybody had seen anything, they weren't letting on.

Below the bridge pool what had once been the mill dam was now derelict, the water gushing out through two narrow guts at either side. Beside one, a heron stooped with a grey and anxious concentration. Swallows and martins were hawking flies over the water, splashing in occasionally.

We made a final check of the cottage keys. It's no fun to arrive back at five in the morning, exhausted and probably wet, to find that the home comforts are all on the wrong side of a locked door.

The tension was high as we walked upstream – this was our first full night on the river, but we knew that there were plenty of sea-trout in, mostly fresh fish at that. The sea is only a few miles downstream and when the fish come they take the stretch at a rush, through the fish pass without touching the sides, and up into the resting pools.

The footpath beside the river runs beneath fine mature trees, beech, oak and sycamore, supplemented by hazel . In places these come right down to the water. Only on the upper beat do the trees recede in favour of wide grassland and arable fields. Where the woodland embraces the river, the hazards to casting are far outweighed by the benefit of reduced light.

About a quarter of a mile upstream from the bridge a pleasant grassy bank overlooks the most productive pool on the beat, possibly on the whole river. Here stands the hut, base-camp for the storage and consumption of victuals, welcome refuge in a downpour. In front of it a rod-stand houses whichever weapon is not in action for the moment. With a dead low river we were both starting with full floating lines.

The plan was to use the first hour or so, while the light faded, to fish the broken water at the head of pools. Here the extra visibility would be less damaging – fatal to attack the calm water of the pool itself without the aid of darkness. This year it was my turn to start on this first-division pool, and Matthew went back downstream to the one below.

It seemed like hours before the light had gone sufficiently to make a start on the lower half of the pool. On the far bank, overhanging trees give way to a ridge of rock which comes in at an angle to produce a classic narrowing tail. On the fisherman's side you step off into quite deep water which gradually shallows until it's all too easy to make an unseemly and disturbing clatter among the stones. As you reach the tail, which has to be fished right out to its ultimate extremity, you have to be extremely careful not to go in too far and find yourself kicking sea-trout out of their lies.

I stepped carefully in, feeling the familiar pressure as the water clamped the chest waders tight against me. Despite a year's absence, the same mildly hazardous boulders were immediately recognizable, as was the very considerable nervous tension. There is a good story of the old man who said that when he was a boy he always ran the last two fields to the river. "Now", he said "I only run the last field." If I ever get blasé about any fishing, let alone for sea-trout, it will be time to get out the carpet-slippers or take up bridge.

The business end of the tackle was a nine foot 6 lb. leader armed with two flies. On the tail was a Teal Blue and Silver, on the dropper a Dark Mackerel. As the week wears on we experiment with others, but tradition more or less demands these on the first night, and very effective they are too.

Down below, the faint glow from the village was just visible. A bat flittered up the pool, and somewhere out in the darkness a heron croaked harshly. In absolute quiet I worked downstream a pace at a time. It was just possible to see the line as it landed – after that everything had to be dealt with by touch.

Twenty yards above the tail, just as the flies swung round there was a violent pull, an explosion of foam at the surface, then nothing. It's a typical sea-trout experience, but none the less disappointing for that. Suppose that's the only chance of the night?

9

A quick check of the flies showed that both were in good order. There's nothing like sea-trout fishing to turn one into a fanatical hook-sharpener. Then it was off down the pool once more.

After another ten yards there had still been no further offer. Then it happened. A heavy pull was followed by a mercifully brief commotion at the surface, then a steady, rather dignified tension. This demure behaviour did not last long. After coming back upstream until it was almost level with me, the fish suddenly charged off very nearly to the tail before performing a shattering leap in what I knew was not much more than a foot of water. I had a very keen vision of the second fly flapping about looking for a rock to snag. But in fact that was almost the end of the show. After that the fish came quietly, and as it turned on its side it was obviously a very good one. Heart pounding (many and many a fish has come unstuck at this point) I got the net under him and staggered ashore. Going up the bank I felt his comforting and impressive weight in the net.

Even in the dark the pale gleam of the fish on the grass showed that it was by a long chalk the best sea-trout of my life so far. In the event it went 4½ lbs, of no consequence compared with those from the big-fish waters, but a good one from this river.

As I gazed and admired, I thought back nearly sixty years to another great thrill, my first fish ever. Six inches of Thames perch, it was, like all perch, a most beautiful fish in its own right, but a real treasure to me then. Like the sea-trout, it was ceremoniously eaten. Like the sea-trout it was unforgettable. I wouldn't want to judge which was the more life-enhancing experience.

The capture of that first little perch was due entirely to my father. Very few father-son relationships run a continuously harmonious course, and ours was no exception. But nothing could possibly detract from his greatest gift of all to me – a love of fishing and a chance to get started on it.

It was perhaps characteristic of his occasionally detached attitude to his children that he was not actually present when that first perch came kicking into the boat.

Chapter One

My father, Walter Pierce, spent part of the 1914-1918 war in the Flanders mud, and the rest, until he was wounded, racketting about in the air over the trenches in a Morane Parasol aircraft which was not particularly safe even when nobody was shooting at it. The Parasol was one of the earliest monoplanes, and looked it. The designer appeared to have lost his faith at the last minute; a vertical peg had been installed in the centre of the wing and from the top of this, stay-wires were attached to all the less stable parts of the structure.

It did possess one advantage, good overhead visibility all round. Below it was a different story, and it was from this angle that a German fighter approached, fired upwards through the floor of the aircraft and hit Father in the right hip. Recovering he manned his single Lewis machine-gun and drove the German off. The following citation appeared shortly afterwards:

Awarded the Military Cross
Temporary 2nd Lieutenant Walter Maurice Pierce,
General List and Royal Flying Corps

For conspicuous gallantry and devotion to duty. Whilst on artillery patrol his machine was attaccked by a hostile scout. Although he was wounded by the first burst of hostile fire, he continued to work his gun, and succeeded in driving off the enemy machine, which is believed to have been severely damaged. When taken to the C.C.S. he insisted on being sent to his squadron, in order to make a reconnaissance report on movement behind the enemy's lines. After doing this he was taken back to the C.C.S. where he was operated on and the bullet extracted. This officer has proved himself a most reliable observer. He has done consistent good work, and many of his reports have been of the greatest value.

The expectation of life either for an infantry subaltern or an airman was in those days measured in weeks rather than months. But when it was all over he found himself, to his great surprise, not merely a survivor, but also more or less in one piece. Having beaten the odds he must have felt, like many another, that the rest of life was a bonus to be enjoyed to the full. He certainly never believed that it was to be taken earnestly or seriously. As for the conventions of respectable behaviour, anyone else was welcome to them.

Nonetheless he had to make a living. Returning to his native place, High Wycombe in Buckinghamshire, he found a job selling furniture, mainly to the large London stores such as Heals and Maples. It suited his outgoing personality and ability to make people laugh. But his threshold of boredom was extremely low, and ways had to be found to enliven, in particular, the humdrum regular train-journey to London.

One method was to climb out of the carriage, which in those days boasted a footboard, and clamber along the outside grimacing at the startled passengers within. He also had a particular antipathy for bowler hats, and once seized one from the head of a perfect stranger and hurled it out of the window. Until the last the stranger was convinced that he was merely the victim of some conjuring trick and that the hat would be returned to him at Marylebone. It was not, and he had to be content with the price of a replacement. These and similar antics are still recalled and recounted to me with pleasure by people who knew him then, (though not, so far, by the man who lost the bowler).

My uncle Wilfred remembered an occasion when Father challenged him for a bet of £5, a considerable sum then, to get out of a restaurant with one of the ashtrays. He was half-way to the door when a familiar voice raised the cry of "Stop thief". Wilfred was equal to the occasion, however. Rapidly explaining the situation to the head waiter, he was allowed to leave the restaurant, and then returned, claimed his fiver, and split it with the waiter.

Father was good at his job, but it cannot be said that he found it particularly fulfilling. He probably should have stayed in the army, for which he always had the highest regard and affection. Undoubtedly some of the people he met, in the Royal Flying Corps particularly, had a great influence on him. It was probably Saundby, later Air Vice Marshall Sir Robert Saundby who introduced him to fishing, which along with cricket and shooting became his greatest love. He also for a time played a pretty good standard of football, and indeed claimed to be the only genuine amateur in the Wycombe Wanderers Club, then described locally as "the worst-paid amateur side in England." As he hurtled down the centre the cry would go up from the onlookers (hardly a crowd) – "Go on, mad 'ead."

He made soccer history, of a sort, at the 1923 Wembley Cup Final when for some reason, before the match had even started, the crowd invaded the pitch. Swept along with them, Father and a friend found themselves becalmed at the centre spot and, having had several pints beforehand, seized the opportunity to make themselves comfortable for the rest of the match. It's doubtful if the centre-spot has ever before or since been similarly christened twenty minutes before a Cup Final kick-off.

Chapter Two

The Buckinghamshire town of High Wycombe lies about twenty-five miles due west of London, in the valley of the little river Wye which gives it its name. In the 1920s it was a long thin collection of houses and furniture factories which was at that time only just beginning to spread out beyond the immediate slopes of the hills overlooking the river. From any point in the town it was only a few minutes walk into the cool airy beech woods on which the prosperity of the place was originally founded.

It is still possible to find in these woods the pits used by the chair bodgers to saw up the beech trees used in local furniture making. The log was laid across the pit. One man stood on top, pulling his end of the cross-cut saw, in this case operated vertically. The other, presumably junior, sawyer stood below in the pit and got covered in sawdust, one must suppose. It all sounds incredibly hard work. The basic product of the small men was the Windsor chair.

As time passed production moved on to a much larger scale. By the time Father was involved, there were some very substantial enterprises including those of Gomme, Ercolani, Birch, Castle and Glenister. Many are still in action today, notably the first two named which produce the G-Plan and Ercol ranges of furniture.

The Gomme enterprise, so I understand, could well have been in part our family business. Father's own father, Tim Pierce, had close connections with the founder, Ebenezer Gomme, who indeed married Tim's sister Alice. But, like Father, Tim was more of a

17

convivial than an industrious nature. Although he worked for the firm, as did Father after the 1914-1918 war, there was never a Pierce holding in the Gomme furniture empire.

My great-Aunt Alice was a kindly though formidable figure. Barry, my elder brother, and I used to make the most shameless formal call on her just before going back to school for each term. He collected a tip of £1, while I got 10/-. The custom lapsed very early in the war, before I graduated to the higher rate.

I never recall meeting Great-Uncle Ebenezer, but his two sons Frank and Ted (Father's cousins) were familiar figures, especially when in the late 1930s we moved into a house in London Road, conveniently placed between the cricket ground and the factory. Barry and I often visited the offices and the woodyard, where the sliced logs lay for years, seasoning. Each plank was separated from the next by wooden spacers, in the same order as in the original log, so that one got the impression of an expanded drawing. The timber was stacked on small trolleys on rails; in due time it was shunted down to the main line and carted off into the factory. We used to visit the workshops with Father, and one of the band-saw experts would take a piece of scrap timber and turn us out a tiny chair, all in one piece.

My maternal grandfather, Ralph Janes, was the proprietor of a different kind of furniture business. Nicholls and Janes produced some of the best hand-made reproduction furniture in England, and were chosen to make many of the pieces for the Queen's Dolls' House at Windsor. Quite frequently someone would acquire perhaps two or three Chippendale or Sheraton chairs, for example, and would commission Nicholls and Janes to complete the set. No doubt many of these pieces continued their lives as antiques. Ralph was considered an expert in such matters. On one occasion he was in a London furniture store when Queen Mary was questioning the provenance of a chair which was being offered as original Chippendale. The manager called Ralph to adjudicate, and was not best pleased when it turned out that Nicholls and Janes had made it.

Ralph Janes's father had been one of the founding partnership, having started on the shop floor. Ralph himself served his apprenticeship as a cabinet-maker, before taking over the firm; I do not remember any Nicholls being in evidence by the time I was old enough to take an interest.

My mother, Muriel, was the oldest of seven children, a loving yet strong character whose leadership among the seven would never, I think, have been disputed by the others. At the outbreak of the 1914-1918 war she was at school at a convent in Belgium. Inevitably, it was she who at fourteen years old was chosen to conduct the English party home, armed with an umbrella, lent to her by the Mother Superior, by way of badge of office. After the war, the Reverend Mother wrote and asked for it back.

Father's own early life is maddeningly obscure, and by the time I started on this book, those who were of an age to tell of it were gone. It seems certain that he never had anything in the way of higher education, probably leaving school at fourteen. There was a period when, according to family legend, he 'ran away to sea.' In fact it was to nowhere more maritime than rural Essex, where he had a spell at (one could hardly say 'in') the landlocked naval training establishment HMS Ganges. There is a relic of this in the form of a leather briefcase awarded to him as a prize in 1912, when he was seventeen.

Another period was spent in the office of W.J. Winter-Taylor, a solicitor in the town, with whose children Barry and I subsequently spent a great deal of time. But Father can scarcely have made good solicitor material.

In 1911 Corporal Walter Pierce of the Boy Scouts (horrors of militarism!) was presented with the Coronation Cup by the Mayor. Around that time he also became the first King's Scout in Buckinghamshire. He must already have been showing signs of leadership and a lively mind.

The most interesting development was when he was commissioned (General List – Infantry) on January 7th 1915. At this stage the war was only a few months old, and the army must still have been officered very largely by regular soldiers, or at least by people drawn from the same sort of social mould. It is a tribute to his personality, ability and, no doubt, charm – which was considerable when he chose to exert it – that from his modest background he gained this commission. The naval experience and his being a King's Scout no doubt helped.

The county regiment was the Oxford and Bucks Light Infantry but I think he served with the Middlesex Regiment, then machine-gunners. Knowledge of these advanced weapons may have enabled him later to transfer to the Royal Flying Corps.

Father married Muriel in 1921. She had apparently been engaged twice before to young officers billeted in the town but why neither of these engagements had gone ahead is not recorded. She was certainly an extremely pretty girl and served as model for a wooden sculpture of a woman's head which is still to be seen in the Oak Room of the Town Hall. Barry was born in 1922, and I in 1925.

Unless earlier volumes have been lost, it appears that Father started to keep a diary in 1924. The first is in a book in which he had originally kept notes of an army training course. It appears to have related to the work of the battalion pioneers. 2/Lt Keltie of the Seaforth Highlanders held forth on road-making, while Capt. Bird of the Sikh Pioneers gave instruction in trenches. The handwriting is clear and neat, and there are some excellent little drawings.

Most of the contents of the diaries have to do with fishing, shooting and cricket. Those covering the period before I was able to join in make fascinating reading, (so indeed do those thereafter – my recollection of events and his are not invariably identical). A few random entries may give some flavour of his style.

July 7th 1925

> "Met Johnson and his keeper. After a slight argument, was invited to fish his pool".

This took place by the little River Misbourne, near Amersham. It was typical of Father that what started out as a minor altercation ended with an invitation.

December 16th 1926

> "Saw HM the King shoot at Lord Burnham's estate. About 900 – 1000 brace shot – HM the best shot of all – killed an extraordinarily high pigeon".

How on earth did he get himself invited to watch?

February 6th 1927

> "To Micheldever with Dove – trout to 3 lbs. Got permission to fish 'when desired' "

July 21st 1927

> *"Kept wicket for the county against Norfolk"*

November 20th 1927

> *"Caught a poacher who claimed he was 'only killing vermin'. In the afternoon Bob Lee, Wilkinson and self went off to poach some of — 's pheasants with a .410 from the car – an outsider and has too many pheasants".*

What was sauce for the goose was quite clearly not sauce for the gander!

April 15th 1928

> *"First Test trout, above Saddler's Mill. About 6 inches.*

May 22nd 1928

> *"Met . . . who was going to buy my walnut trees, but he was so drunk he could not talk sensibly. Made himself amusing, then unpopular at the* Bel and the Dragon"

February 16th 1929

> *"The usual sort of Saturday when there's no shooting or fishing".*

February 17th 1929

> *"Skating at Shardeloes. Took about fifty tosses and sprained wrist".*

April 22nd 1929

> *"As usual when I appear on a trout stream there was a howling*

wind. No fly, of course".

October 28th 1929

> *"Cricket club dinner – oh dear!"*

October 29th 1929

> *"Had a go at the pug in the boxing booth at Marlow Fair and knocked him out in the second round".*

The hangover obviously can't have been crippling.

December 21st 1929

> *"Lump (his flatcoat retriever) demonstrated retrieving in Brecon High St. at 11 p.m.".*

August 15th 1930

> *"Shared in a murderous piece of work at Saunderton – 42 rabbits out of a piece of wheat. I was hit on the leg, another man on the chin and it was a miracle that nobody was shot properly".*

November 27th 1930

> *"Nicely fooled by a merchant seaman who got me to promise not to run him in if he told where a partridge was that had hit the wires and dropped. I agreed, and he replied 'In my pocket' ".*

October 14th 1931

> *"Lump put away – knew nothing. She dined on hot partridge and roast potatoes. Shall never have another like her".*

He didn't.

April 2nd 1932

> *"Two large grayling on a spinner – returned."*

April 10th 1933

> *"Elected member of MCC"*

December 12th 1934

> *"Surprised to see — (an intelligent man and a member of MCC too) shooting owls".*

September 23rd 1938

> *"To see Dick Rowley's shoot in the morning. Took it at the rent he suggested, i.e. nil!"*

Father's work load was apparently not an onerous one. Very few weeks passed without at least two sporting outings of one sort or another. Talking to the people who, though not strictly contemporaries, knew him well in the between-wars years, it is apparent that he was a sought-after companion, witty and entertaining. These are the sort of qualities which are invaluable in business, and clearly he could earn what he felt he needed without keeping his nose to the grindstone all hours, six days a week, which was essential for many in those days.

This book is about fishing rather than an intense and searing exposé of a son's relationship with his father, full of psychological insights and so on and so on. The relationship nevertheless did exist, and did have some effect on the fishing, so a short account is perhaps not out of place.

In talking of the 1930s and 1940s we are going back fifty years, and there's no doubt that since that time family relationships in general have changed. In those days, no matter that there were numerous exceptions, the general 'culture' was that wives and children were both subordinate to the *paterfamilias*. He supported the household; everybody in it supported him, put his whims and fancies first, and generally toed the line. They did not, of course, have to like it, but the incidence of rebellion, tension, feelings of injustice, resentment and general uproar cannot surely have been any worse then than they are now, when the laid-back approach is more or less standard. Certainly, most of the families with which we were acquainted seemed to be run on much the same lines. Quite simply, that was how it was. Authoritarianism, at present outmoded, was the name of the game.

There are still people about who remember Father. Their memories will be of someone intelligent, witty, eccentric (sometimes to the point of wild irresponsibility), extravagant – good fun, in a word. Certainly he was all these.

No coin is the same on both sides, however. The reverse of this one showed autocratic, quick-tempered and demanding aspects which could be quite remarkably trying in the home. For my mother it was hard to see the free-spending extravagance directed more outside the household than in. If it came to a choice between buying the Sunday joint or a train ticket down to the Lambourn there would be little doubt about the outcome. It would be absurd to say that we were ever hard up, at least not by the standards of that time, but steady and secure our finances certainly were not. My elder brother Barry and I were spared any detailed knowledge of this, but an undefinable anxiety certainly made itself felt at times.

Much more strainful for us was the fact that Father expected us to be in attendance far more than was convenient, desirable or (most serious) than was demanded by the fathers of our friends. For example, whenever he went to London for the day, we had to see him off and meet him again in the evening. It baffles me to this day why he should have wanted this but the attitude was fairly consistent. If we were about, we were expected to be on hand and ready for whatever projects he had in mind.

The snag for one trying to build up a youthful head of resentment was, of course, that these projects were often highly diverting – cricket, fishing, shooting or whatever. On the whole these occasions outbalanced such boring ones as walking up the town to watch him playing snooker at the British Legion.

Where fishing and shooting were concerned we were expected to spend a long apprenticeship of bag-carrying, beating, watching and listening before we were gradually introduced to taking part. I can now see that this at least was wholly beneficial, especially in the shooting field where safety is so important. A raw youth, armed by his fond papa and decanted into the action without experience is a menace to himself and all around.

If my attitude to Father had to be summed up in one word it would probably be 'wary'. The very last suitable epithet would be 'relaxed'. Apart from the fact that he expected a great deal of us, there was always the possibility of a violent explosion.

All that being said, the fact remains that he was generally good company, and certainly things were never dull when he was around. In any case, the easiest of all people to forgive is one who stays cheerful and that, generally speaking, he did. Not many of us can score a hundred per cent in all departments and at all times.

In our household one strange ceremony used to take place each morning. A good deal in advance of his time and genre, Father installed two bathrooms in our house in the London road, one, of course, for him, and one for the rest of us. By no means an early riser, he would usually be installed in clouds of steam while the rest of the family were having breakfast. On the chair by the end of the bath was a wind-up gramophone; at intervals there would be a bellow from upstairs and one of us would have to sprint up and revive the dying clockwork by a brisk burst on the handle. We had very few records, and the repertoire consisted largely of repetitions of "Miss Otis regrets she's unable to lunch today" and "Standchen" ("Wonderful, wonderful, Jesus is to me-hee"). These were occasionally varied with the justly renowned Frank Crummit singing "The Song of the Prune" or "Abdul the Bulbul Emir".

No early start was called for, because on the days when he was in fact earning his bread, there was no question of leaving for London before the 10.10 train. This was known as the beer-wagon, since it had a restaurant car, and a regular small coterie would gather here to play whist on the way up. No such facility was available on the early evening trains back to High Wycombe, the resulting boredom giving rise to some of the antics already described.

Demanding and trying as Father frequently was, Muriel obviously loved him dearly, and waited on him in a way that now would probably be thought disgraceful even by women who would not consider themselves to be raging feminists. This does not at all imply a lack of spirit. On one occasion Father electrified the changing room in the cricket club by revealing red-painted toenails as he donned his white socks before a match. Apparently Muriel had been incensed by his refusal to rise in good time from a snooze on his bed. She was painting her own nails, and threatened to carry on with his toes if he didn't get up. Father fatally nodded off again and got the treatment. But it was, after all, a period when a father's, or husband's, word was law to an infinitely greater extent than it is now. Her own father was at least as autocratic. His pet hate was a salt-celler that wouldn't pour, and meal times were frequently interrupted by a savage roar and a crash as the offending pot was hurled into the fireplace. A huge conical plastic affair with a hole as big as a sixpence eventually solved the problem.

One of Muriel's wifely duties was to gather the food plants for Father's butterfly breeding. He was a good amateur entomologist, and built up a first-rate collection in a handsome cabinet. This has long since disappeared and no doubt had to be sold to relieve one of the periodic financial crises which became ever more frequent during the war and subsequent austere peace. His breeding activities started with common species such as tortoiseshells and peacocks, then moved on to swallowtails, one of which is still preserved in an ingenious though fairly unattractive scarab in the form of a brooch. His greatest interest was in the clouded yellow and he spent a great deal of effort in trying to produce a specimen of the pale variety called *Helice*. He never succeeded.

In those days the Chalkhill Blue was regularly to be found in places about the Chilterns, notably on Kop Hill near Princes Risborough. Accoring to Father, dealers from London made a deliberate attempt to wipe out that colony in an attempt to keep up the value of their specimens.

He was, indeed, interested in and knowledgeable about many aspects of natural history, and was keen that Barry and I should follow suit. Part of our education, and a highly enjoyable one, was to spend two weeks, just before the 1939-45 war, camping on the rearing field of the shoot at Bradenham in which Father had a gun. We were there to help Sidney North, the keeper who himself lived throughout the most critical weeks of the rearing period in a shepherd's hut, something like a gypsy caravan but a good deal smaller and plainer.

Father was one of the few guns in the syndicate who took an interest in the out-of-season activities on the shoot. Apart from the camping episode, all of us used to spend a lot of time with North ferreting rabbits, helping with the bits of forestry with which he was also involved, checking tunnel traps or whatever else was going on. On each visit we took a tribute of an ounce of Players 'No Name' tobacco – 9d an ounce.

Sidney North could be described, as my Aunt Kate described Father – he was an 'original'. Apart from his keepering he could build, carpenter, and cut hair. His barbering kit was kept in a blue cloth bag printed 'Barclays Bank'. It was a most pleasant experience to sit outside his hut on a herb-scented Chiltern bank, while he snipped away in the sun. He was also a fairly tough egg who, according to legend, took on the neighbouring keeper of Sir John Dashwood in a bare-knuckle fight on the green at Bradenham. Sir John's man was taken home on a hurdle, but that, of course is the version according to Sidney.

He taught us how to snare rats, hangman style, with a bent-over hazel wand, and how to kill rabbits and grey squirrels with his powerful Webley air-rifle, a formidable weapon. With it, we also used to lie in wait for pigeons coming down to drink at a lovely pool in the beech woods.

Pheasant rearing in those days was totally unlike present systems. Broody hens were set on the eggs, each in its barred hutch. Each hut had a peg and a string attached to a leg ring on the old hen so that she could take some exercise at intervals. The chicks gradually ranged further afield; as they became more adventurous Barry and I would have to go out and tap down the hedges to bring them back in to feed. Usually we would find some mushrooms by the way, which with a rasher or two of bacon and eggs from the no longer broody hens made a superb breakfast in the open air.

The food for the pheasant chicks was cooked in a giant pot – the convenient and scientifically designed pellet had yet to be introduced. Into the pot went wheat, eggs, flaked maize, rabbit meat, a meat residue called greaves and many more ingredients which I've now forgotten. It smelled delicious.

It must be confessed that 'old North' (as we thought of him – he was probably about 45) could fairly be described as an old-fashioned type of keeper, in that absolutely anything with a hooked beak was shot or trapped without mercy. Even kestrels got it in the neck, and indeed, on that sort of open rearing field a local kestrel could do a great deal of damage. I was once sent down to lie in wait for one which frequented the corner of a new planting of firs. It was a very hot day and I was soon asleep. I woke to find the kestrel hovering almost directly above me. I slowly raised the double-barrelled folding Belgium hammer-gun, a .410, but just could not squeeze the trigger. It's a matter of pride now, but then I felt distinctly ashamed at having let North down.

He was certainly no respector of persons, and gave Father and me one of our best laughs ever during a ferreting expedition. For once, one of the other guns came with us. He had no experience of the game, and found it all far too slow for his liking, particularly when one of the ferrets failed to reappear. North set about the business of retrieving it, gutting a rabbit and placing the paunch close to one of the holes. Then he began fanning the scent down the hole with his hat, a malodorous affair which would probably have done the job on its own. All this was done with great deliberation, to the irritation of the novice ferreter. Most unwisely, he started to offer various useless advice. North eventually straightened up from the hole and said – "Mr — sir, you don't know bugger-all about it, sir!" And he applied himself once more to the job.

Mrs North produced a vast range of powerful, indeed almost lethal, home-made wines. Those made from roots were outstanding. A slug of her parsnip wine was once administered to keep me warm during a long spell of stationary duty as a 'stop', and had me practically bow-legged. Father walked out one Christmas to see the Norths and leave a present. After he had been plied with some of Mrs North's finest he set off home, but became unaccountably tired and sat down to rest on a milestone. Two hours later he was still sitting there like a garden gnome, the home-made wine having entirely removed his power of locomotion.

Father expected both boys to learn about shooting by starting at the bottom as beaters. It is a policy strongly to be recommended. We became fully proficient, and were paid at the full rate of 7/6d a day, well worth having at that time. More to the point, we learned what was going on over the hedge, a great aid to safe shooting later on.

Both the parents were great lovers of dogs, and we had some splendid characters at various times. Best of all was the flatcoated retriever, Lump, whose demise was recorded earlier. She was obviously a first-rate working dog, and was probably responsible for some of the invitations to shoot which Father received. Less satisfactory, professionally speaking, was the labrador Belle, who though loveable was pretty hopeless. This is no doubt why she subsequently became my first dog. Like most labradors she was addicted to water, and enjoyed nothing better than crashing about the Dyke, an ornamental water in High Wycombe, annoying the moorhens. If a stone was thrown into a couple of feet of water she would almost completely submerge in pursuit of it, leaving just a black behind and waving tail above the surface. She always came up with a stone, sometimes the right one.

Belle came to an untimely end on the railway line. She was not killed outright, and the local policeman called on poor Father to bring his gun and shoot her. He was on the spot before he realized that it was his own dog.

We also had an old spaniel called Pickles. Father took him, on at an advanced age from Sir Edward Durand, who was moving to where he could no longer keep a dog. Pickles was a good enough old sort, but always made it quite plain that it was something of a come-down for him to join us.

Next came Pooch, a black and white smooth haired terrier which Father had somehow been given, and passed on to me when I was about thirteen. Pooch was by no means the first creature to arrive at home in such casual fashion. Father once came into my room in the middle of the night, opening a cardboard box and poured out a two-foot snake. Although it was not much use for stroking or cuddling, Barry and I got quite fond of the beast; it used to be carried round the house, curled around the forearm, browsing on woodlice or spiders. Eventually it disappeared and was found during the following spring-cleaning, flattened and desiccated under the drawing room carpet.

Pooch was extremely active after rats and rabbits, but was subject to hysteria, then much more common. The first time he fell into a whimpering, foaming fit I thought he'd gone mad, and shot up a nearby tree. He eventually grew out of it. When the war came he was the only dog in the family and was allowed to come away with me to Devonshire, to where the school, Dover College, had been evacuated. He was in lodgings with a gamekeeper, but eventually, sadly, had to be put down when I left. Pooch had the not uncommon canine habit of reacting to certain kinds of music, in this case the mouth-organ. Father kept one around the house for the special purpose of providing this entertainment. As we played it, Pooch's head would slowly rise, as if involuntarily, until his muzzle was pointing skyward and the lips formed into an 'O'. He then produced an unearthly drawn-out howl, fit to chill the blood.

After the war, Father had one more dog, another flatcoat and again called Lump. I had her sister, Sally. Neither had the opportunity or the training to be of any use in the shooting field, but were good company. Lump was spoiled rotten by both Father and Muriel. She never had any pups, and did not at all care for anyone else's. When Sally had a litter of by-blows by a neighbouring sheepdog, Lump disassociated herself from the whole affair; if approached by the only pup we kept she would leap into the nearest armchair and sit there quivering. Sally, on the other hand, was highly maternal. Although I only kept one of her own pups, cross-breds being very had to place, she was immediately saddled with four Great Dane pups whose mother had turned savage. She reared them without turning a hair. After that she still had some milk, and an orphan lamb, being reared on the bottle, used to suckle her vigorously. We often wondered how it turned out as a sheep.

One of Father's few tedious characteristics was a tendency to practical jokes. Curiously he seems to have had this in common with a far more distinguished airman, Lindbergh, as recorded in Ludovic Kennedy's rivetting and horrifying book *The Airman and the Carpenter*. Perhaps there is some connection with flying. On the cricket ground once, I was sent off to take a message to 'Mr Beetle' whose name of course turned out to be Bugg. Another time he despatched me with a basket of apples to be taken home, and then arranged for a local policeman to intercept me and question me about where I'd got them. None of it seemed very funny, even then, but at least he took it in good part when he himself was victimised.

Chapter Three

Our small house in Manor Gardens, High Wycombe, the first I can dimly remember, was taken some time in the 1920s purely on the strength of the Hughenden stream which ran along the end of the back garden and gave a good fifteen yards of fishing. It was dammed up, netted off and stocked with a few trout. One day, Father reported that a pike was making unacceptable inroads, and must be stopped. My elder brother and I, then aged about seven and four, found nothing odd about this although the stream was barely too wide to step across. Under instruction we rigged up a night line. For a couple of nights nothing happened. On the third morning (tribute to Father's feel for a dramatic build-up), puce with excitement, we found a jack pike of about 3 lbs on the end. It didn't put up much of a fight; in fact, it seemed to be dead, exhausted no doubt by its struggles during the night. We were triumphant, Father congratulatory; it was a thoroughly satisfactory affair all round.

Inspired by his success Father then got us to dig a pit-trap in the garden; gullible as we were, even we found it hard to accept the dead mouse that turned up in it the following morning. But it was years before we learned the truth about the pike.

The little river Wye in High Wycombe was earlier famed for its trout – much of the ova which went out to make the initial stocking of New Zealand waters was reputed to have originated there. Its tributary the Hughenden stream was pretty good too. Sadly, by the time I was old enough to take an interest the water in the town was already in decline through pollution. The head waters remained pure, but much plagued by drying up. One year we mounted an exciting rescue operation to net trout from the Hughenden stream and transfer them down to a point lower down where the stream was still running. The whole business with nets, dustbins, lorry and so on, the splashing about, the sense of urgency, was all extremely entertaining.

The stream into which the fish were to be turned ran beside watercress beds which were fed by artesian wells. The water poured out from vertical pipes about a foot high, clean pure and cold. Father persuaded an enormous friend, Jimmy, that with his weight he could stand on top of the pipe and stop the flow of water. So he could; but as he stood there, the pressure must have built up, and the moment he tried to step off again, he was flat on his back among the watercress.

The state of the river in High Wycombe between the wars must have been a sore trial to Father. It was bad enough for me, as a small boy forever poking about trying to spot just one trout. I dipped out a dying fish with a landing net in about 1936 which must have been about the last. The cause of the pollution was factories of various kinds discharging their all into what had been by repute, one of the finest trout streams in England. Tom Thurlow, a local architect had not so long before taken two fish of over 4 lbs., both of which are still in existence in their cases. Miraculously, or rather I suppose by a lot of hard work, the river is now once more clean enough to hold trout. Due possibly to abstraction it carries nothing like the water that it did. Even so, the offspring of trout breeding successfully in the headwaters have filtered downstream. The Thames Water Authority has done some re-stocking, and it is now possible to see trout rising within a few hundred yards of where we lived. One of the best-populated places is right behind the cricket ground. Father would have been delighted.

Father was a good cricketer, notably as a wicket-keeper. He captained High Wycombe, a strong club side, and played a good many out-matches for the M.C.C. Sadly he never gained a regular place in the county side where the wicket-keeping place was held for many years by W. B. Franklin. Father believed that, be the bowler fast or slow, the right place for the keeper was right up behind the stumps. As a result he received some mighty blows, and I remember once seeing him stretched out cold in the pavilion, with an ice-pack on his head. It was a hot day and people kept tiptoeing in and stealing bits of his ice to put in their drinks. He finished with a nice cool, damp rag.

Father's diaries start, briefly, in 1924, and became reasonably full thereafter. The early years refer almost exclusively to fishing, shooting and cricket; other activities hardly rate a mention. Things changed as sickness, injury and family troubles became intrusive in the 1940s.

The first cricketing reference is:

July 19th 1926

   "Made 62 for Jack Page against Brondesbury".

This is a surprising entry, because although he could make runs on occasion, he generally batted very well down the order.

Clearly fishing and shooting were his main obsessions at this time, for there were very few mentions of cricket thereafter until:

August 1st 1927

> *"Played for County two days last week against   Norfolk   and did well at the wicket".*

This is confimed by a card, sent from the Junior Carlton Club by Walter Franklin, congratulating Father and thanking him for turning out at short notice.

In 1931, either the cricket considerably intensified, or he became more conscientious about recording it; quite probably it was then that he got the captaincy of the High Wycombe club, or started to aspire to it. Also, he notes that on June 9th he was elected as a probationary member of M.C.C. During June, July and August twenty-two days cricket were recorded.

Cricketing diary entries:

June 13th 1931

> *"Beat North Middlesex by one run in the last over, 197 to 198. Last four wickets fell in seven balls for no runs. I caught two, stumped one and had no byes. Made six and then trod on my wicket."*

June 23rd 1932

> *"Wycombe v. Brookfields 19 not out. Caught two, stumped one and had two good catches refused. A terribly bad finger from Friday's match, standing up to field the young pro fast bowler".*

This problem with the hands was clearly nothing unusual. At several places in the diaries the writing becomes barely legible for several days when Father was obviously writing left-handed having broken yet another bone in his right hand.

May 16th 1936

"A great game at S. Hampstead. After losing 5 for 60 we got 300. Teddy Beeson and Harry (Harry Janes, my uncle) *had a grand stand and I managed as No. 10 to get 22 and stay while 71 were put on for the last two wickets. They got the runs for 9 wickets in the last over.One man was bowled and didn't go. Umpire at bowler's end said the ball came back off my gloves. Umpire at square leg said he was not stumped, and also gave him not out, so he stayed and got another 20!"*

June 6th 1938

"Played Indian Gymkhana – lost badly. Bowled in the second innings and got 3 wickets, including Jahangir Khan who got 161 in the first innings."

May 29th 1939

"My XI against Wycombe. We lost and I broke a rib."

July 6th 1939

"Played at Kingshill. Got a frightful crack on the nose from Emery. Bled for a week, then to hospital for a week."

One of his wicket-keeping wounds necessitated a period of convalescence at Bournemouth, to which he was accompanied by my mother and me. Piscatorially it was a fairly barren scene, but he soon found that on Boscombe pier it was at least possible to watch people sea-fishing, a sport of which he knew extremely little. One day I stumped beside him along the pier to the very end, where we found an enormous and formidable woman clad in the sort of leather coat favoured by the late Field- Marshal Goering. She was kitted up with an extremely stout rod, large reel, and on the end of the line the traditional Christmas-tree paternoster, about a pound and a half of assorted ironmongery. She took up her stance to cast, and we watched respectfully.

There was a powerful heave, and the Christmas-tree took off in a magnificent parabola, to plummet down into the calm sea at a distance which looked like about a quarter of a mile. Father was highly impressed."Jolly good cast!" he called out. The woman turned to him, face contorted with fury. "You bloody fool" she grated "I hadn't got it tied on properly".

As far as I know Father only ever made one attempt at sea-fishing. This was during one of the family holidays which came round all too infrequently, since all his holiday was normally taken in odd days for fishing, shooting or cricket. We took a cottage somewhere in West Wales presumably because of the rumour that salmon tackle could be employed to catch bass in the surf, thus enabling something at least to be salvaged out of what was otherwise likely to be a sport-free week or two. The whole affair got off on the wrong foot. Because the cottage was some way from the pub Father took the precaution of asking for "a dozen Bass" to be waiting in the cottage when we arrived. Instead of the desired bottled beer, twelve beautiful fish, fortunately not enormous, were waiting in the sink when we eventually trailed in. Humiliatingly, these were in fact the last bass we saw on shore on the holiday. Although they were undoubtedly about, all efforts failed. At one point Father, a strong swimmer fortunately, ventured well out to stand among the breakers and lay about him with a salmon spinning rod which simply would not give him the distance when he stood on the beach. He reported that he could see bass in the waves as they passed, but take they would not.

For us as a family, indeed, the sea is clearly not our forte. Years later, also in Wales I found bass coming right up to the beach where a tiny stream fell in, their spiny dorsal fins actually breaking the surface, but I only got a few fruitless casts in before they passed on.

Far worse befell when years later I stayed with my uncle Eric, Muriel's younger brother, at a cottage at Porth Gain in Pembrokeshire. Eric had served something of an apprenticeship with Father and, like him, was interested in any sporting venture. We hatched a plot to lay a trot-line in the little harbour. This had been built many years before to ship out stone but was now only used by a few part-time fishermen and a very occasional tourist. We set up an amateurish rig with about twenty hooks on it. This was to be laid out on the sand at the edge of the water at the lowest part of the ebb, baited with bits of mackerel. The tide would then come in, and when it receded again, there would be our fish like a line of laundry, pollack, flat-fish, who knows, perhaps even a sea-trout.

It was not to be. As we laid the line out, there appeared one of the infrequent visitors accompanied by his dog. Before we could even think of the danger, we had our first catch, about seventy pounds of frightened and angry Alsatian well-hooked through the tongue. It was appalling. The owner promptly tried to extract the hook simply by pulling it. Stopping him, I cut the line; although order was restored we were left with an unpleasant situation. The only thing was to cart the dog off immediately to the vet. As the dog owner's car disappeared up the valley, our venture was abandoned in disorder and we trailed back to the cottage, nerves shattered, never to attempt it again.

The next day a postcard arrived addressed to 'The Man who caught the Alsatian at Porth Gain'. This was delivered unerringly to me, the village grapevine having made the whole affair a matter of public knowledge within minutes. Mercifully it appeared that the hook had been extracted without difficulty and the dog was well. Nowadays the owner would no doubt have sued me.

Despite his lighthearted, indeed anarchic, approach to fishing (and to life), Father was in fact a good and successful fisherman in his selected branches of the art. It seemed to be his view that you don't have to be solemn to be serious, something which might well be recommened to a few of the heavyweight pontificators in the angling press. I cannot imagine what he would have thought of the correspondence columns of modern angling papers where so many people now write in to castigate each other's views both savagely and contemptuously. He would probably have found it hilarious that people could take a recreation so seriously, especially one in which so little can in any case be proved for certain. It never fails to amaze me that someone can take such a dogmatic line in a matter about which he can subsequently be shown to be totally ignorant. There was a splendid example a few years ago when a closely-reasoned letter demonstrated to the complete satisfaction of the writer at least, that to turn a pack of otter hounds over to mink-hunting was simply not practical. Needless to say the following issue of the journal concerned carried a letter from someone else whose otter-hounds had just killed their forty-third mink of the season.

After the late 1930s, except in its head waters, the little Wye ceased to hold anything but sticklebacks and, curiously enought, still some crayfish. These are normally extremely sensitive to pollution, but for some time after the trout had all gone it was still possible to find a few by wading and turning over the stones. The sticklebacks so far as I know never did disappear, and were quite worthy quarry for small boys, especially in spring when the cock fish got themselves up in a magnificent livery of red and emerald green. Temperamentally they are a good deal like perch, bold and aggressive. We used to catch them on a cane and a piece of cotton. No hook was called for; you simply tied on the worm, which had to be of just the right size, about an inch and a half long and not too fat. When this was lowered anywhere near the sticklebacks they would come charging out to attack with great vigour. Once one had a fair hold it could be swung ashore and the worm gently pulled out of its maw. Quite often we would get two at once, one on each end of the worm.

Once we graduated to more serious work, the only place available was the Thames. Effectively we had a choice of two or three places, all easily accessible by bus, since we never, or almost never, had a car. Upstream was Marlow, site of the weirpool and inn. I pass through Marlow from time to time now, and am always struck by how little the centre of it at least has changed. A pleasant High Street leads up past the riverside church, and the road is then carried over the river by a delightful suspension bridge like none other on the whole river until it reaches London itself. Below the bridge lie the weir and its attendant lock.

Marlow was extremely active with pleasure boats during the summer, from rowing-skiffs to cabin-cruisers. At least it seemed so then. Now the river groans under the weight of traffic in summer with the accent heavily on large motorised craft. Gone altogether are the elegant electric canoes which used to glide about in merciful silence.

A peak of activity came with the annual regatta when people poured in from all sides and the whole town apparently took the week off. From the fishing point of view this was the time to operate downstream at Bourne End or further yet at Cookham. It was here that my first attempts at coarse fishing were made. It was a long time before the smallest success was registered.

The earliest expeditions were made under escort by my mother. Father knew virtually nothing of such fishing and wasn't very interested in learning. However, he armed me with reasonably appropriate gear, and the first attack was on. At Cookham the river was dominated by Turk's boathouse, headquarters of the 'swan-upping' foray which occurred each year to take a census of the swans, most of which belonged to Her Majesty the Queen. Mr Turk masterminded this expedition which involved a lot of chasing and splashing and some very angry swans.

The boathouse was beside the bridge on the Berkshire side, and from here a ferry ran to take foot-passengers over to the island downstream of the bridge. The ferryman was an artist with his boat, an extremely stout affair like a very large dinghy which would easily carry seven or eight passengers. The nose always pointed upstream. The crossing to the island was downstream, and the ferryman simply stuck the nose out into the current and with only a few strokes of the oars the whole load would make a traverse and draw against the little landing-stage on the far side. Coming back the performance was even more impressive. This time he would have to pull strongly but he never even glanced round. The boat would move unerringly to the home landing-stage and at the last minute the starboard oar would be shipped and a large, brown, horny hand would reach out and steady the craft for disembarkation. The fare was twopence each way.

The island had been formed by the channel cut when a lock was installed, and was full of bleak, dace and small chub. No doubt there were plenty of other species, but these were what were visible, and these were what we fished for. The great Thames bait of the day was hemp-seed, despite dark rumours that the fish would all become drug-addicts. It had to be boiled until the white inside just peeped out through the seed-coat, and was extremely hard to put on the hook, for a small boy at least. Alternatively we used bread-paste, which in our case was always bullet-hard after a short immersion.

For hours we watched the unresponsive float. I don't know what we were doing wrong but the results were minimal. After we had trailed home from about the third unsuccessful mission, Father decided the time had come to do something about this before my enthusiasm was killed permanently. Barry for some reason was never particularly interested in fishing in the first place.

In those days the Thames still had professional fishermen who made a living by acting as boatmen, guides and advisers to amateurs. These men, of course, were key figures for much of theThames trouting, but this time the objective was different. One man at Marlow operated a punt from the weir corner by the inn, The Compleat Angler, and he was engaged to take me and a friend, Marcel Winter-Taylor, out for some serious coarse fishing. It was a tremendous outing. We both must have been about ten years old. We spent half the previous night sorting out the gear, and in the morning got the bus over to Marlow and reported to the weir corner. It was a fine summer day and the river looked its best. Each half of the punt was equipped with an old chair, legs shortened, but these were for later use. We were made to sit in the bottom of the boat out of harm's way while the boatman paddled us sedately over to the tail of the weir where the water ran about four feet deep over clean gravel. Pointing the punt directly downstream he rammed in the first ryepeck, a steel-shod pole, and tied up to it; then, as the other end drifted round he put in another, and tied to that. We were moored broadside-on across the current. Only then were we allowed to take our seats on the chairs.

Next, he produced an enormous rake on a pole about as long as the ryepecks, and with this vigorously raked the gravel just below the boat. This was by way of groundbaiting, and obviously released a coloud of various good things such as caddis and shrimp. Then it was time for us to get going with our fat celluloid floats, well shotted, size 12 gilt hooks-to-gut and small red worms. What a contrast from our previous pathetic efforts! On the first swim down there came a thrilling bob-bob then off went the float and in came a perch. It wasn't a big perch, but a tremendous thrill all the same. There cannot be a much handsomer fish and certainly not to me, then. Marcel was also in action, and the sport continued flat out until it was time to go. We had nothing of any size, but a good variety of perch, gudgeon, roach, dace and little chub. Father met us at the inn on our triumphant return and we celebrated the success.

The episode taught me a valuable lesson, though it wasn't apparent at the time. If you have a child who shows an interest in fishing, it is vital to make the first expedition in circumstances where success is as near as possible certain. That the catch may consist only of little perch or gudgeon is not important. Provided the float bobs, and there comes that electrifying tug, you've probably made a lifetime enthusiast. There cannot be many better turns for a child than to give him a love of fishing, something he can enjoy all his life until he's too old and grey to stagger to the waterside. What's more, he can go on learning and getting better at it just as long as he continues to fish.

Many years after my own initiation, a friend, John Holloway, asked me if I would start off his small son, about eight years old. The professional Thames fisherman was long an extinct species, but the weir corner at Marlow was still there, and still, no doubt, full of little and maybe not-so-little fish attracted there by the handsome eddy and by the crumbs left by the feeding of swans. The Compleat Angler was by now a very grand hotel indeed, but when I explained the situation I was very kindly given permission to conduct the lesson there.

It was a highly convenient place for the job. A smooth landing stage made it easy to avoid getting hooked up, and there was only a couple of feet of water flowing steadily past. Overhanging trees gave background cover, and the whole business could be conducted right under the rod top. As for me long before, the action was immediate. There were no perch for this was the period when a horrid disease (now happily receded) had almost wiped them out. But we had lots of gudgeon and dace, an occasional roach, and quite a decent chub. Tim was nearly as excited as I was.

Wading on the weir was an obviously highly competent and well-equipped fisherman making a serious attempt on the barbel. After half an hour's continuous tiddler-catching Tim remarked pityingly "Look at that poor chap – not a thing, and here I am catching gudgeon, dace, roach – the lot!"

Not all of the many lessons I learned in that weir-corner had to do with fishing. Another professional who at one time operated from here had only one leg, the other being the traditional Long John Silver wooden peg. We were loading up to go out one day when he slipped and gave the good leg a thorough wetting. I laughed, and immediately got a smart and painful clip round the side of the head from Father, who rather unfashionably for those days wore a heavy wedding ring. Nothing was said at the time but I afterwards tried to explain that it wasn't because the man had a wooden leg that I found it amusing. Anybody falling in would have been funny – especially Father, though naturally I did not add that. "Of course," said Father, "but does he know that?"

It was on the Thames that Father taught me to cast a fly, catching bleak and dace. It was the worst possible practice for trout-fishing because the strike had to be made like lightening. The lock at Cookham was one of the best places, and indeed Father claimed to have caught a 1 lb. dace in the lock itself. It was probably a small chub; with Father, no story ever lost anything in the telling. There was a high footbridge which was particularly good fun because of the excellent visibility. Standing up there the technique was simply to dangle the fly a foot or so above the water and then watch for a patrolling dace, or occasional chub to come within range. The fly was then dibbled up and down and was not very often ignored. If the fish was other than minute it was then necessary to retreat to the bank before it could be landed. The bleak often ended up as spinning baits but everything else went back.

For us boys the absolutely favourite fishing spot was the old horse-punt at the downstream end of the island at Cookham, below the lock. Originally this had been used to transfer the horses which pulled barges. They came up the far bank, and the transfer operation is one which I would very much like to have seen. Presumably the exercise had to be repeated at the top of the island, but no horse-punt survived at this point. The punt must have been about 18 feet long and wide in proportion, and made an ideal fishing platform, apart from the fact that it provided cover for a permanently resident shoal of perch. We used to take our sandwiches and bottles of vile fizzy drinks to make a social day of it. Perch, which are excellent eating, were always killed and taken home, deeply shocking to most of today's fishermen no doubt, but in those days the fishing pressure was immeasurably less than it is now.

Every now and again Father would appear after trying for a trout in the weirpool and we would have to make way while he spun all round the punt which had occasionally been known to harbour a big trout. The chances that it would still be around after we had been there for an hour or two seemed slim – we were not the quietest of fishermen.

One day for a change he was experimenting with one of the new American plugs which had just started to appear on the market to the mingled amusement, amazement and horror of the English fishing public. This particular one was called, I think, the Heddon River-Runt Spook. Bright coloured, bedangled with numerous huge treble hooks, possibly jointed, it was about five inches long and certainly ran no risks that a fish might not observe its passing. It was extremely expensive.

Father worked it cunningly all about the punt but it did not behave like an ordinary spinning bait. Before long he'd managed to get fast somewhere on the underside of the punt. As he tried pulling from different angles he got crosser and crosser, muttering under his breath. My friends very sensibly held their tongues but as he was my father I felt entitled to laugh. Does one never learn? Next minute I was made to strip off and go in after the new toy. It was easy enough because it was only just under the edge of the punt and the water was reasonably warm but came unmistakably under the heading of being 'brought down a peg'. Regular application of this was then considered an essential part of the upbringing of small boys.

I thought about this years later when bobbing about off the coast of Pembrokeshire in a dinghy with two of my own sons. That particular foray was to pick up our sole lobster pot, buoyed beneath its makeshift float, a half-gallon plastic lemon-squash container. The pot was a collapsible one marketed by Mr Leakey, of Settle, in Cumberland, whose exciting advertisements for all kinds of fishing gear then appeared regularly in the angling press. I once rang him for advice about how to fish the pot from the shore, rather than a boat. Having told me all about it he finished, dramatically . . ."and take a sack – you'll need it." It never came to that, though certainly through no fault of the pot.

In Pembrokeshire we caught an occasional edible crab and an interesting assortment of other marine life but never a lobster. It was only towards the end of the holidays that someone more worldly-wise pointed out that other summer visitors in the district included numerous young and early rising skin-divers.

Even so, raising the pot was always a thrill. After yet another disappointment we were heading back when the boys started fooling about and eventually, one oar was lost overboard. My eldest son, Matthew, was made to follow it in his underpants under the admiring gaze of walkers on the cliff-top path.

Father's cricket took him here and there about the country and very frequently the family was taken along to watch. I don't recall ever being given much choice in the matter. Certainly in those days it was less fashionable to allow the little personalities to develop at their own sweet will and children's activities were more frequently organised for them. Conversely, if we did put forward some project that was seen as worth-while, such as a fishing expedition, we were given more freedom than many children enjoy now to put it into practice. It was of course much safer then than now for children to be out and about on their own.

Sometimes it was possible to fit in some fishing or at least fish-watching activity. One such opportunity was at the Odney Club in Cookham. This was on a backwater of the Thames and, although it provided tennis, cricket and other games, nobody seemed to bother to fish. We were not allowed to do so either but spent hours lying with our heads just sticking over the bank to watch the really splendid roach that the water held. We learned quite a bit about fish observation there, how closely you can watch if you keep still and low, how to use light and shade. There was a dreamy quality about watching these beautifully-marked fish slowly drifting about their business among green weeds and over golden gravel.

Although Father was really only interested in trout, salmon and very occasionally pike, he certainly did not despise coarse fishing, – it was just a matter of his personal taste. He encouraged us boys to fish for anything that swam, and because he could not advise us in the matter of, for example, roach, went out of his way to find us other mentors.

One of these was Jack Topp, a master Thames roach-fisher. He used to do a bit of umpiring on the High Wycombe cricket ground. He presumably had some occupation other than this and fishing, but if so I never knew what. I was sent off more than once with Jack. It's always a pleasure to watch anybody doing anything really well, and

Jack in action on the roach certainly qualified. For a start all his gear was immaculate, one lesson I'm afraid I've never learned. He used a roach-pole, which went out of fashion subsequently for about thirty-odd years and has now made a come-back. Float tackles were kept on handsome wooden winders, made up ready. The casts were of silkworm gut rather than nylon. For the water he fished at Bourne End he used very light gear (or what seemed so then) with a quill float. The fashionable hempseed was his usual bait but in the early autumn he would also use elderberries. What I remembeer most was his ability to spot and react to the most infinitesimal bites. Seldom did the float do anything so crude as to go under. A slight dip or a hesitation was enough for Jack to strike delicately and in would come another roach or dace.

Twenty years later, on my honeymoon, I came across a Majorcan Jack Topp. The harbour at Palma held quite a lot of mullet. The more casual fishermen went for them within the harbour walls and the small ones they sometimes caught would go for soup along with all the other assorted little ones. The serious mulleteers fished on the seaward side of the wall, and we sometimes went along to watch. A reel was seldom seen, most people fishing with a fixed line on a rod made of two or three sections of bamboo cunningly cut so as to fit together with natural suction joints. But by far the worst deficiency was in the end gear, generally crude and with an excessively large hook, and in the unimaginative style of fishing. It seemed to me that the mullet were generally near the top, but everyone just carried on fishing near the bottom with about six feet of line under the float.

Not so Jacismo Topp. As soon as we saw him, old Jack came to mind, not only in the workmanlike way all his tackle was disposed and handled, but because he'd clearly put his mind to the job and was fishing quite differently from the rest.

His float was shotted at the base, with the small hook only six inches sor so beneath it. He had two pots beside him, one full of breadcrumbs and the other containing a well-made soft bread paste. First he would draw the hook through the paste to arm it with a ragged little chunk, then dip the bait in the breadcrumbs. Thus with each cast he produced a tiny puff of groundbait, with his bait in the middle. We watched him catch several mullet up to nearly a pound, which may not be a big mullet but was about four times the size that anyone else had, apart from the fact that he was catching a great deal more than they were.

I had already acquired one of the local bamboo rods and, although we were leaving the next day, I was determined to see if it were possible to emulate this master. We had to leave for the airport at 10 a.m., but before seven we were out on the harbour wall with the rest. As always, the sea looked very large and empty but I got to work and after an hour the continuous mini-groundbaiting seemed to have brought round a fish or two. Suddenly the float darted away and I was into a mullet which looked about 1½ lbs. Alas for the absence of a reel! The contact was dramatic but brief; I tried vainly to swing him sideways, but after one mighty wallop on the surface we parted company. Honour was satisfied, all the same. The incident caused a gratifying stir and we could hear the news being passed round the harbour as we bolted off for the plane.

When I hear people talk about fishing calling for patience I wish they could have had a day out with Father. Patience was something of which his stock was minimal, a characteristic which my children tell me is for sure hereditary. Fishing might have been 'the

53

contemplative man's recreation' to Izaak Walton – not to Father. In the weir corner if there was not much action the day would be enlivened by a foray in the punt. Ostensibly the reason would be to go off and try this or that corner but in reality it would be for the thrill of a little joust with the water as it crashed through the 'lion's mouth', the centre opening of the weir. All the gear would be firmly stowed, boys disposed strategically about. Then, with all paddles going we would set off like a war canoe through the quieter water below the weir apron. The idea was to reach our not very impressive maximum speed just as we took the lion's mouth sideways on. The roaring current snatched the punt and hurtled it down to the tail. The punt was so solid and stable that there can have been virtually no risk of trouble but it was exciting stuff all the same. It lent some added point to the professional boatman's account of how when he found a body in the weir he always towed it in to the Buckinghamshire side, because that county's coroner paid a better honorarium than the Berkshire man by way of reward.

January 18th 1931

> *"Joe and Lynford Davis caught a dead man while spinning at Bourne End. He had hands and feet tied together."*

Chapter Four

It is notorious that our memories of days gone by are always golden: the summers were hot and sunny, the food tasted better and so on. But I'm sure that though the Thames today is unquestionably purer down at the London end, it seldom has the glorious green vinously aerated character that I remember from early days after the Thames trout. It was highly exhilerating to stand by the weir, or by one of the eddies at the tail, to smell the water, and to watch the bubbles and flecks of foam bustling about. The sound of the roaring weir contributed to the atmosphere.

In the very early spring now it is still possible to recapture some of all this, but all too often the water seems a little more brown, a little more lifeless. The much heavier boat traffic must be one of the causes. Thames-side is still a marvellous place to be, and an enlightened Thames Water Authority is now following in the footsteps of the Thames Angling and Preservation Society of the 1930s and stocking the weir-pools with trout. Once again it is worth turning out in April, where there is the best possible chance of finding the river as it gloriously used to be.

Some time around 1930 Mr A.E. Hobbs wrote a classical little book, *Trout of the Thames*, which recognised Thames trouting as an art quite separate from the normal thing. The principal methods were livebaiting and spinning, the latter invariably and almost as a matter of dogma with a dead bleak mounted on a special flight of hooks in a manner calling for some expertise. Only occasionally was the fly called into use. Between the two world wars the Thames Angling and Preservation Society regularly stocked with trout to supplement the native stock. They grew to very heavy weights, well into double figures, but were never plentiful. The weirs were always well patronised by both trout and fishermen, but on the main river the trout took some finding. Enthusiasts like Hobbs and Father maintained a keen intelligence system among boatmen, lock-keepers and other regular habitués of the river to obtain reports of where a trout was feeding. Once one was located, siege would be laid, and this would be assisted by the almost clockwork regularity with which the fish would feed. Occasionally Father would leave one of the boys to watch the spot, and it was a dramatic moment when the shoal of bleak suddenly scattered, leaping in all directions, with one unfortunate eventually disappearing in a heavy boil.

The respect with which A.E. Hobbs was regarded in Thames trouting matters is reflected in Father's diary entry for May 9th 1929.

"Marlow. Reappearance of the otters, or at least one of them. Hobbs of Henley also fishing, so there is apparently a good fish there."

For a few years in the 1920s, Father fished enthusiastically for Thames trout.The only diary entry for 1924 records a total for the year of 17 trout totalling 38 lbs. 5 oz., the best fish being 3 lbs. 5 oz. This was his first season of trying for these superb and idiosyncratic fish, and he obviously made a tremendous start. It is clear from subsequent entries that anyone who wanted a Thames trout had to be prepared to work for it; pike and perch usually got there first, and did at least liven up the long intervals between trout.

April 10th 1925

> *"To Marlow. Took 14 jack (pike) and a perch and lost a good trout. He took a silver Devon, but jumped in the fast water and was washed off."*

April 24th 1925

> *"Marlow. 2 jack only. Nearly fell in the Lion's Mouth. Met Major on way home who told me of being smashed up at Abingdon by a huchen or very large trout of 14 or 15 lbs."*

In the 1920s there was an introduction to the Thames of huchen, a type of non-sea-going salmonid native to the Danube, among other European rivers. Nothing seems to have been heard of them for many years.

May 5th 1925

> *" . . . on the last run round the weir hooked a nice well-built trout of about 2 lbs. on live minnow and landed him. It was remarkable that I felt him plucking with about 80 yards of line out all round the corner of the weir."*

June 10th 1925

> *"Marlow weir. Took a nice trout of 2 lbs. 12 oz. on a live gudgeon. A great fight. My winch fell off . . . had to sit on the net-handle and guide the fish over."*

June 23rd 1925

> *"Marlow weir. Took a trout of 2 lbs. 5 ozs . . . something bit part of his tail away. Applause from a Count ? who weighed it for me*

in the Compleat Angler."

Numerous blank and uneventful visits were recorded. Father kept trying the Thames at intervals up to the outbreak of war, but many other fishing and shooting forays diluted his previous whole-hearted attention. He did however collect a best fish of 6 lbs. 10 oz. in Marlow weir, and another of 5 lbs. 6 oz. Both these fish were set up in glass cases, but unfortunately the bigger of the two eventually started to sag most unbecomingly and was disposed of. The other I have now, one of the prettiest trout imaginable.

One other Thames trout incident is recorded, of which, mercifully, I have no recollection at all.

May 6th 1934

> *"Roger hooked a trout fishing in the weir corner by the Compleat Angler, and lost him. Burrows got him later on – 5½ lbs!"*

One of Father's favourite places, well suited to his companiable and convivial nature, was the corner of Marlow weir beside which stands the aforementioned famous inn, the Compleat Angler. We would occasionally be allowed to take the rod while he retired to the bar. Livebaiting with minnow or gudgeon was usually enlivened at least by out-of-season pike and perch. One day a rich friend joined Father and they both eventually went off to the bar, handing into my charge an extremely expensive split-cane rod with associated gear to the same standard. To my horror one of the pestilential swans which infested the river flapped up on to the apron of the weir, taking my line with it. After dithering feebly for a while I grasped the nettle and with a mighty heave (tackle was fairly substantial in those days) tumbled the brute back into the weir. By good luck, everything came free. Father was proud of me, but we didn't tell the friend. We could never understand the popular enthusiasm for swans, arrogant and bad-tempered beasts that they are. The cob who owned the weir-pool regularly drowned his offspring if they did not clear off as soon as they were fledged.

Non-fishing friends loved to turn up at the corner of the weir to watch with drink in hand, frequently offering unsolicited and unsound advice. One day Jimmy, the victim of the artesian well, arrived, about 18 stone in weight and bibulous by nature. He spent most of the morning, when not in the bar, throwing in little stones around Father to simulate rising trout; he didn't realise that most Thames trout wouldn't be caught dead 'rising' in such a piffling manner. It was a hot spring day, and after lunch he tired of the game and retired to sleep on the sloping deck which formed one end of the punt. Father waited until he was (non-too-silently) well away, then quietly slipped the mooring and paddled gently up to the sill of the weir. A last hard thrust with the paddle rammed the end of the punt under the sill. About a hundred gallons of refreshing river came surging in to give Jimmy's nerves a health-giving jolt.

Jimmy was a sport and took this and many similar incidents in good part. He certainly made my evening once when we were coming back from a cricket match and stopped at what in the 1930s was called a roadhouse, or gin-palace. Swimming pools were not so common then, but this place boasted one, and furthermore served dinner at tables disposed elegantly about the pool so that diners would be entertained by the swimmers while eating. Jimmy, whether by bet, dare or threat was persuaded to go off the top board, fully clothed. His enormous bulk hit the water like a bursting bomb and sent most of the contents of the pool over the diners. They didn't care for it, and our party had to leave in a hurry.

Below the bridge at Cookham the river divides into several streams, including the lock cut. The weir is nearest the Buckinghamshire side. Somewhere below there is another little weir or sluice which in those days certainly was privately-owned. Father somehow gained access to this, and one day set off to fish it, accompanied by my Uncle Harry, my mother's other brother. He was a good shot and played more than sound cricket and hockey, but fishing had so far been outside his orbit. This would be the opportunity to learn, perhaps even to be helpful.

It was a warm May day, and there had doubtless been a visit to the Ferry Inn before operations began. While Father began to ply his live minnow about the eddies, runs and corners, Harry disposed himself pleasantly in the shade to watch.

Livebaiting tackle for Thames trout then consisted of a two-yard gut trace of 2X or 3X. A similar thickness of today's nylon would afford very considerably greater strength. This had to be soaked before use to remove its initial brittleness, and damper-boxes could be bought for the purpose, round, hinged, and equipped with layers of felt. Most of us used Player's tobacco tin with a screw-top, full of bits of old shirt. The trace would be armed with a size ten treble hook, and a shot placed about a foot and a half above it. . The float was never anything but a wine-bottle cork slit down the side for insertion of the cast.

The selection of this float was almost ceremonious, if not superstitious. These particular trout, so the dogma ran, were of such superior eyesight, such immense cunning, that a common red-topped float would be fatal to success, insulting indeed. Even the unaltered cork would arouse suspicion; it must be trimmed about with a razor blade so that it would look just like any bit of flotsam that might come bobbing past. When the cast had been drawn into the slit a shaved matchstick was stuck in to jam it in place. It was an extremely inefficient rig; the objectives would have been better met by boring a hole through and threading the line before pegging with the matchstick. We lost lots of corks, but the float certainly made a brave sight in action.

On this occasion it was an hour before Father's cork suddenly vanished into the foam and bubbles. It was another rigid tenet of belief that Thames trout always seized the bait with extreme violence. The strike this time as always, was instantaneous and a nice fish was on. Harry was galvanized from sleep by a loud bellow from Father, and came galloping over with the landing net. To those who understand the matter the operation of a landing-net is simple, if not necessarily easy in actual execution. The net is sunk, the fish drawn over it, the net raised. Unfortunately it hadn't occurred to Father that Harry might not know any of this. As the fortunately well-beaten fish was drawn to the bank the order was given, "Right, when you're ready." Harry reached out and seized the cast about two feet above the fish, carefully lifted the trout clean out and then dropped it into the net which he had held out above the water like a frying-pan waiting for its egg. Mercifully the fish was only about 2 lbs. and everything held. Harry's younger brother Eric went on several subsequent fishing expeditions but I don't recall Harry ever making a repeat trip.

Cookham was the scene of another incident as a result of which Father gave me about the only moral precept that I can now recall receiving from him. He was in the Ferry Inn with a friend when an

61

aggressive individual for some reason started to needle him. All attempts at pacification failed. Father attempted the soft answer, friends intervened, the landlord tried to lay down the law, but nothing was any good. The man was determined to pick a fight. Eventually honour demanded that they went out into the yard to settle the matter. "All right," said Father "get your jacket off." The aggressor, by all accounts a hefty one, slowly and menacingly shrugged his jacket over his shoulders. When both arms were still irretrievably fast in the sleeves Father, who was a fair boxer, gave the man a most dreadful blow in the *solar plexus*. This, on top of the beer he'd been putting away, did the fellow no good at all. As he writhed breathlessly on the cobblestones, Father decamped. Afterwards he told me, "If anyone goes out of his way to pick a fight with you, you're not obliged to stick to the Queensberry rules." So far I haven't had to use this undoubtedly sound piece of advice.

About half a mile below Marlow weir a small stream falls in on the Berkshire side. This had made its way along under the hanging beechwoods on the hills. At Bisham, perhaps a mile above the outfall, there was a small pool beside the road-bridge. Bisham Pool was reputed always to hold a big trout or two as a result of their making their way up the stream at spawning time and being unable to make their way back when the winter's flow died away. Father had told me such inspiring tales of this place that one day I cycled over there, five none too easy miles with a bait-can of live sticklebacks. These we could catch at home and it was by no means certain that minnows would be catchable on the spot.

The pool, which has now vanished altogether through the straightening of the banks, was no more than twenty yards long and ten wide. The stream entered under the road bridge and made a couple of rather feeble eddies, then speeded up over the gravelly shallows at the tail. The far bank was well tree'd, but on the fishing side there was just one large thorn bush overhanging the water. I had an old greenheart rod and a thin silk line which must have been mounted on a trout fly reel because we had no others, except for salmon. The fixed-spool, or 'threadline' reel was still a novelty and widely regarded as highly reprehensible, little better than a poaching device, definitely unsporting. "They land the fish for you," we told each other, never having even seen one.

The obligatory camouflaged cork was soon floating motionless in the middle of the pool. It was late May, all the winter water was long since gone, and there was very little flow indeed. There was no wind either, and the whole tackle looked ludicrously obvious. Even my unfortunate stickleback was able to produce a few miniature wavelets around the float.

I don't think I ever really believed in the possibility of a trout; a little jack-pike perhaps. But suddenly, and as violently as the legend demanded, my cork simply vanished out of sight in an instant. The reaction when I tightened up was absolutely terrifying. The trout made one tremendous rush and leaped straight into the branches of the thorn bush, giving me one splendid if brief view before it flopped back into the pool having shattered my poor gut cast. Twelve years old or not, I wept, and should probably do so now if the same thing happened again.

A week later Father returned from a visit to Marlow. He had made the short extra journey to Bisham to make enquiries at the pub. My fish had been caught, he reported, and weighed 3½ lbs. My hook was apparently still in it, almost certainly a detail added from his fertile imagination to round out the story satisfactorily.

Catching the livebait was in itself an entertaining pastime. For minnows we used a trap made out of a bottle, broadly on the principle of a lobster pot. This was baited with bread. In the right place the minnows would soon be round butting their little blunt noses against the glass until they found the entrance. Once there was one captive, others would soon follow. It was extremely seldom that any other fish was caught by this method.

For a more mixed stock of small stuff the one-legged boatman at Marlow used a drop-net. This consisted of the rim of an old bicycle-wheel with a piece of brown minnow-mesh stretched loosely over it, a weight attached to the centre. A loop of string allowed a piece of bread to be fixed to the inside of the net, opposite the weight. He never needed to go further than the weir corner. The net would be dropped in close to the landing-stage, and a handful of crumbs put in close by would soon attract the customers. Ten minutes were enough, five probably, and the net would be smoothly but gently lifted to display a wriggling mass of minnows, gudgeon, dace and the fry of roach, chub and who knows what. Very often a little perch, attracted by the bustle, would also be found. Only the minnows, gudgeon and dace were considered tough enough to be of any use, or a roach if it was big enough for pike bait; everything else went back.

When bigger baits were needed for pike-fishing they were caught by rod and line. The backwaters seemed to be the favourite places for this, which we generally did under the supervision of the boatman. Father could somehow never be bothered with this but liked to watch, and we had some marvellous sessions catching quantities of roach and dace. For the boatman these were a saleable commodity, though the market of course was not unlimited. None the less he enjoyed having the unpaid labour of small boys, and we benefited from his knowledge of where to go and how to set about it.

For pike, current thinking had it that any unusual livebait would be infallible. Thus in a small lake with no bleak, the use of one of these would ensure success. Nobody ever produced any evidence of this – we just believed it. A goldfish, of course, would be a stranger in most waters. Very early one morning we set off on a piking expedition. It was only just light when our companion turned up in the car to collect us. We had a bait-can full of water, but no baits, and I assumed that these were either to be caught when we got there (always a chancy business) or bought from one of the boatmen. The town was all asleep as we went through, and after half a mile or so we drew up outside a quite impressive house. Father handed me a net and the bait-can.

"Just nip in and dip out a few goldfish from the little pond on the side lawn," he said. "The chap here is co-operating in an experiment to see if this goldfish theory works. And," he added, "be quiet – we don't want to disturb him."

Without much difficulty I extracted some six-inch fish and was nearly back at the car when an upper window flew open, and there was a shout. Father urged me into the car and we were off.

"I couldn't hear what that chap was calling out," I remarked.

"Probably wishing us luck," said Father. It was no doubt a judgement on him that the pike that day ignored the goldfish and everything else we tried.

Nowadays I don't livebait any more, and as time went on I don't think Father would have done so either. He always used to let a bait go if it had not been taken after a short while. Nature is, of course, red in tooth and claw; every second of every day some creature is being consumed by another, probably alive. All the same, I am no longer happy to tether a fish to await its doom. It quite made my flesh creep once to read a fishing writer cheerfully describing how he knew that a pike was approaching his live roach because of the sudden agitation of his float. The logic of these misgivings is probably dubious, but there are plenty of other ways to catch fish and in these busybody'ish days it's as well not to give any ammunition, however spurious, to the anti-fishers.

Father was incredibly relaxed, as it now seems, about giving us boys our heads in our own doings. (In anything to do with him, on the other hand, discipline was intense) So from quite early ages we were quite often off camping, or messing about on the river. My best friend's father was much the same. He owned a very handsome old launch, the Lotus Lily, which was kept at Bourne End. It was about eighteen feet long, with an inboard engine, the sort of thing made for decorous river parties at Henley, ladies with parasols, thin sandwiches and bottles of hock – that sort of thing. With us it had a rather more stimulating time, and it amazes me now that both fathers (whether or not mothers were consulted I don't know) were happy to let the two of us take this craft out on our own from the age of about twelve onwards. Perhaps, like the father in Swallows and Amazons, they felt that 'Better drowned than duffers – if not duffers, won't drown.'

We had a lot of fun in the Lotus Lily. Generally speaking we lived up to the trust extended to us, although on one occasion we nearly came unstuck. An expedition upstream with our two elder brothers ended at the Compleat Angler, where the two great men went ashore for a drink, leaving us to wait in the boat. It seemed a good joke to maroon them and we were soon offshore in the weir, enjoying their angry cries from the bank. It finally dawned on us that we would have to return eventually, and that Nemesis would inevitably strike. It did, and we both got a tremendous cuffing. It turned out that their cries had been of warning as well as rage; the weir was very full and had we turned the Lotus Lily broadside on we could easily have capsized her.

At Bourne End, where the Lotus Lily was berthed, a small stream, the Abbots Brook, drops in just beside the boathouse. It ran down through the gardens of a number of very expensive houses, and even boasted a tiny lock. At the mouth of this stream Father once brought off a very unusual feat by catching three Thames trout in one evening on mayfly. I don't know whether the river still has a mayfly hatch, but it happened sometimes then, though the fly was never as thick as it is on, say, the Kennet. Possibly these fish were not truly Thames fish because the Abbots Brook was occasionally stocked and these might just have dropped down. But, I never heard of anyone else bringing off a similar feat. Another time when he was fishing at the same place, a three-pounder, not hooked, jumped clean into one of the boats.

Armed with a fly-rod (the Allcock's Hexacane) I once took a canoe up the Abbots Brook. It was a chalk-stream in miniature, with its starwort, ranunculus and golden gravel. Dace and small chub were everywhere. I paddled up past the well-manicured gardens of the houses, many of which had splendid timber boat-houses with decorative balconies and summer-house. It must have been early morning because there was no-one about at all apart from a patrolling bull-terrier which barked at me from the bank. Eventually I found a trout. He was only about ¾ lb. but occupied his lie like any Test 3-pounder, rising in a relaxed way from time to time. I tied up the canoe and crept up to cast to him from the cover of the bankside shrubbery, probably something exotic from Tibet.

Had the stream been heaving with fish I should no doubt have given up and moved on after failing to get the fish in the first ten minutes, probably less. It wasn't, so I plugged away, changing flies, 'resting' him from time to time as convention demanded. The casting cannot have been too bad because he kept feeding and eventually made a mistake. It was quite tense work for a moment or two among the weed-beds, but eventually I spooned him out with my hooped wooden landing net and knocked him on the head.

Only then did I become aware of a presence behind me, and turned to see an elderly lady, extremely elegantly turned out. It's probably just in my imagination that she was carrying a parasol.

"I've been watching you for the last twenty minutes," she said. "You've done very well. And now," she continued, "kindly remove yourself, and that trout. You're trespassing."

The numerous angling magazines of today are crammed with the most intricate detail of various pieces of tackle and the permutations of the methods of rigging them. Father was more of the style of an old Welshman I've read about, Dai somebody or other, who fished his native streams successfully with just one set of tackle which had to make do for the fly, spinning or worming. He didn't go to quite that extreme but there was certainly one spinning rig which served for salmon, trout, pike or bass. The only difference was in the end gear.

The rod was a stout split-cane of about 10 feet, the remnants of which I still have somewhere. Any self-respecting rod then came with a spare top, and when eventually both started to spring at the seams, my eldest son Matthew shortened one to about a foot and we carried on using it for holiday sea-fishing. The reel was a most substantial affair of the Nottingham type (centre-pin, that is, of course), put together in brass and wood by someone who meant it to last. It did. It was made in about 1922, and was still in use (though an extremely reluctant revolver) in 1976 for pike-fishing on the Kennet. It then disappeared, possibly stolen but more probably left on the bank, where it may well be buried in the undergrowth to this day.

The line was stout and green. The last yard or two had to be tested by vigorous jerking before the trace was attached, and often a piece could in fact be broken off before you came to healthier line. It was always a mystery to me why only the end bit rotted, but perhaps it was more a matter of wear and tear.

Then came a gut trace, for salmon or trout, or a wire one for pike. Leads were either the spiral Jardine sort which went on the line itself, or pierced bullets with a wire loop which could be run on to the top eye of a swivel.

For Thames trout the lure was either a bleak mounted on the set of trebles called a 'Thames flight', or else a Devon minnow, invariably silver. There were two variations on the standard pattern. One had a bulbous round head; the other, the Reflex Devon was flat-sided so that in section it would have looked almost rectangular. The theoretical basis for this was never clear, but Father greatly favoured it for a while. The only thing I ever saw caught on it was a minute perch only an inch or two longer than the spinner. We were moored at the tail of the weir and Father was in some sort of muddle at the reel end. To while away the time I dangled the minnow up and down by hand below the boat. It dived nose-first, then rose vertically and looked like nothing in nature, but the perch, displaying the admirable ferocity of the breed came roaring out and charged it. It was just as well the fish was not more substantial, or I might have been overboard.

Father's problems at the reel were almost certainly caused by the dreaded 'over-run', all too easily achieved. As the bait and lead sailed out, (no inconsiderable weight between them) it was necessary to have a finger ready to stop the reel revolving just as the bait hit the water. Failing this, as the line ceased its forward motion, the reel would go on spinning, hurling off coil after coil of line which would cling and tangle in the most remarkable way.

The great drawback with this sort of gear was that it was quite impossible to fish without lead or even with a very light bait. It was heavyweight stuff or nothing.

As the spinning tackle was multi-purpose, so were the fly rod, reel and line which were also used for live-baiting. One of the reels is still with us, now armed with a sinking line, and comes out once a year for a go at the sea-trout. The lines were all silk, and had to be greased well if they were to float. Like all the lines of those days they had to be run off the reel to dry at the end of each outing. The rod was an extremely good split-cane which had been presented to Father by a friend, Rupert White, for whom he had acted as best man at some time in the twenties. Rupert White was still a member of the Piscatorial Society, though no longer an active one, when I joined the Society in 1975.

Provided you were fishing from a boat or the weir corner this rig was in fact perfectly adequate for live-baiting. The line floated under its own steam, if greased, and the fact that there was a cork and live minnow on the end instead of a fly did not worry the rod in the least. Like the salmon rod it eventually started to spring due to wartime neglect, and finished up cut-down for pike-fishing, where it handled a sprat or a spoon perfectly cheerfully.

The last time the salmon rod was in action was on the de Lank river on Bodmin Moor in Cornwall. We were on a family holiday and made a foray to the moor for walking, fishing and picnicking, according to taste; my wife, daughter and three sons all came along.

The de Lank river was fishable simply on a River Authority licence which then cost about twenty-five pence. All styles were allowed, but my youngest son Edward, about seven years old, had then not graduated to fly-fishing. We were short of rods so the old salmon rod was brought out, the length in fact being quite an advantage since it made it possible to stand well back yet still dangle the worm into interesting places. Stern instruction was given about the necessity to keep out of sight as far as possible.

It was a boiling August day, and before long most of us had given up. We gathered for the picnic. Only Edward toiled doggedly on. I could see him about fifty yards away standing bolt upright on the bank of what was certainly a promising pool.

"Look at that blessed boy," I said to the others. "Did I not drum it into him that he should keep out of sight? He's standing there like a lighthouse."

Inevitably at that moment, all was action. The line tightened though it would be an exaggeration to say the rod bent. After a brief unequal struggle a trout of a good 7 oz. sailed past Edward's ear into the heather.

We had a post-mortem later and discovered that the pool contained one absoslutely enormous underwater boulder shaped like a coffin. Clearly the fish must have been lying on the other side so that effectively, a fisherman on the bank was completely out of sight. Edward claimed to have realized this all along. There is a good deal of his grandfather in him. Recently we were dealing with weed on a river. I was out in a pool in chest waders, dragging and heaving, while he stood on the dam below helping the wads of weed on their way down to the weed-rack. It seemed to me that I was perhaps getting dangerously near the Plimsoll line, but it was difficult to see so I called out to Edward "How close is it to the top of my waders?" "Don't worry," he called back, "I'll let you know if it goes over the top."

In three or four years of intermittent trying, before the war came along and distracted everybody, I never caught a Thames trout, and I don't think Father ever tried again after 3rd September 1939. The Thames Angling and Preservation Society had by then not stocked for a good few years and the trout were probably scarcer than they had ever been. But now that the Thames Water Authority is once again putting in trout, I've armed myself with a weir ticket and hope that after all these years it may be possible at last to put one in the book. Livebaiting is still allowed, with minnows only. The idea of once again working the hand-carved wine-cork float about the eddies is attractive from the nostalgic point of view, but perhaps it will be more exciting yet to try a sinking line and a big silvery sea-trout fly in the fast water. In the lower weirs there might well be a chance even of a salmon now.

I last spent any significant amount of time on the Thames in 1943 while waiting to get into the army. A strange Home Guard unit called the Upper Thames Patrol had been established, and I got myself transferred to this from the school platoon when I left. That also had been a fairly curious unit. The maths master, 'Aunty' Dale commanded the local company, the headmaster served under him as our platoon commander, the school handyman was platoon sergeant, the corporals commanding sections were all boys, and the rank and file a mixture of boys and masters, the latter more ancient than modern for the most part. Because of the training provided by the school Officers Training Corps we were in fact rather efficient, and it was something of a shock to join the Upper Thames Patrol and find that the whole lot appeared to have only one proficiency badge between them. The unit's function was something to do with guarding bridges, but the patrol routes took in most of the riverside pubs as well. I joined largely because they were reputed to sport a rather glamorous naval-style peaked cap rather than the unprintably-nicknamed side-cap. Needless to say this headgear was dropped shortly before I joined. They were a cheerful lot and I enjoyed my brief spell with them. Our rifle range was on Cock Marsh, on the Berkshire side of the river at Bourne End, and conveniently placed for the Ferry Inn. The Marsh frequently flooded, and it's the only time I've ever had to get from the firing-point to the butts by dinghy.

Father managed to wangle himself back into the army shortly after the outbreak of the war. He was then in his mid-forties and in none too good nick, not least from several mighty blows from cricket-balls but was none the less highly indignant at finding himself in a staff job in London. But at least the air-raids provided that excitement which, in any guise, was always his preference over routine. He was the only person I ever met who seemed genuinely to enjoy the bombing, and he certainly never set foot in an air-raid shelter throughout the war.

He came down one Sunday and met me at the Bourne End Ferry Inn after Home Guard parade. We walked down the towpath to the other Ferry Inn at Cookham. As the bridge came in sight there was an explosion of flying bleak and a swirl as a big trout struck into them.

"One of these days we'll come back and have that one," said Father. But we never did.

Chapter Five.

It's quite clear that in his early years of fishing, trout were Father's first love. The Hugenden stream at High Wycombe ran through the park of what had been the house of Benjamin Disraeli, M.P. for Wycombe, a beautifully clear water, small, but with excellent trout. The whole area is now largely open to the public, with playing fields. Like the little Wye it has a tendency to dry up. Since this last happened, however, it has not been restocked and if it were, the relentless pressure of large numbers of predatory small boys might make it difficult for the population to hang on.

Quite how Father obtained permission to fish is not entirely clear. My maternal grandfather, Ralph Janes, served for many years on the Town Council including a term as Mayor. There must inevitably have been a good deal of contact with the household at Hughenden which may have provided the necessary introduction. But in any case Father was always a great believer in simply asking for permission, on the undeniable grounds that the worst one could get would be a refusal. Whatever the negotiations, he succeeded.

The lower end of the water was only a couple of hundred yards from the little house in Manor Gardens, scene of the night-lined pike. Most of the holding water was provided by a series of little dams, the remnants of which are still there. From such a miniature affair the trout of 1 lb. 12 oz., the best the diary records from Hughenden, was a good fish.

The pool where he caught it was a most attractive place,

surrounded by trees and with a small island in the middle. The last time I saw it was a few years ago when my friend, Norman Gold, a professional photographer, was commissioned to do some work for a company manufacturing gumboots, waders and the like. He press-ganged me not only into finding a photogenic site but also into modelling the gear.

I spent some time climbing into various types of boot and wader and going through the motions of putting a fly over water which quite certainly contained no more than sticklebacks, a slightly dispiriting experience. When the catalogue subsequently appeared the only pictures it contained from this session were from the knees, or at best the waist, down – not a very exciting modelling debut.

Also concerned with the Hughenden fishing was Arthur Clarke, a leading solicitor in the town. Indeed, although the fact is not recorded, he may well have been the actual tenant on the water. Father, however, obviously took a keen interest in the management of the water.

December 24th 1927

> "*Three tries after the heron at Hughenden – no luck. Over Micklefield – no luck. Over the farm – no luck. Over the Sewage Farm – no luck. But an amusing day all the same. Arthur Clarke promised me some trout fry.*"

December 27th 1927

> "*Got the heron before breakfast. Saw him from the road, sitting just below the Island and made a successful stalk to within about 8 yards. Poor brute had a broken leg which had not healed.*

Decermber 28th 1927

> *"Netted the Hughenden stream with the Clarkes and Chivers. Got about thirty big trout and spawned 5. Arthur Clarke gave me some thousands of eggs.*

Maddeningly, we hear no more about these eggs and how they were employed.

In 1929 there are references to two further netting expeditions which between them yielded some 500 trout from this tiny stream. This was the rescue operation already referred to, when the stream was drying up. The trout were put in to the Wye below High Wycombe, for whose benefit is not recorded. But in any case, the stream below the town was already deteriorating then, and the fish may well not have survived.

The Hughenden stream contained nothing but brown trout. In the 1920s, rainbows were far less commonly stocked than today, although the Bristol Waterworks Company was giving a strong lead at the Blagdon Reservoir. The view was quite widely held that it was useless to put rainbows in streams since they would inevitably disappear downstream unless there were fish-proof obstacles to hold them, not particularly easy to organise. Before long people started to get a bit braver about this, and one pioneer was only a few miles away at Great Missenden. He was John Brazil, proprietor of a local company with large interests in butchery and various meat products, pork pies and so on.

He controlled a good stretch of the Misbourne, another little Chiltern stream which ran down from Great Missenden to Amersham and eventually fell into the Colne at Denham. Very near the headwaters there was quite a substantial pool, and it was here the headwaters there was quite a substantial pool, and it was here that Father took me one day in about 1933 to see trout-rearing in operation. It was in fact more a matter of growing them on, because I don't think they actually hatched any. It was certainly a most exciting spectacle when John Brazil's man appeared at the pool side and started to feed. This was long before the days of scientifically manufactured and nutritionally balanced pellets. The fodder was plain minced meat, dark red in colour, so probably beef, though presumably horse was also a possibility. Either way the trout loved it. They started to gather as soon as the feeder appeared, long before the first handful was dished out; then as the meat went in, the water fairly boiled. I'd never in my life seen so many trout at one time.

Once they reached about ¾ lb. they were put in to supplement the existing stock of browns at various places down the stream which was well-bushed in places and provided tricky fishing. The bushes, however, gave plenty of cover for fisher as well as fish, and it was here that Father showed me the fascination, and the usefulness, of careful reconaisance. Wherever there were reflections there was good visibility, provided you got the angle right, and since then I have never failed to get a lot of enjoyment out of creeping into position to observe a trout which is quite unaware of being spied on.

One of the more agreeable fishing places was behind the Red Lion at Little Missenden where the water widened to form a shallow pool. We were there one day when Father hooked a little brown trout about three or four inches long. He'd only fetched it back about a yard, when another trout which looked well over two pounds shot out and grabbed the little chap crossways on, as a pike would. Father immediately gave some slack line, and we awaited developments, hoping that before long the big fish would turn the victim and take him in head-first. Whether or not it sensed somehow that all was not well, the trout simply sat there, unmoving; the troutlet kicked from time to time, and still the captor sat there. Eventually Father's patience, stocks of which were always minimal, ran out; he started to put on gentle pressure, hoping the fish might hang on until the net could be slipped under it. With a pike it might perhaps have worked, but not this time. After being towed in for a yard or two, the trout simply let go and we were left with only the little trout, looking distinctly second-hand.

In a hatch-pool of the Lambourn a few years ago I saw something which persuades me that had Father waited long enough, he might have had that Misbourne trout. It was in October, and I was about to try for one of the excellent grayling in the pool when I saw something pale slowly gyrating in the eddy at the head. Crawling up to the bank I looked over to see a rainbow trout of about half a pound firmly gripped just behind the head by a brown trout of certainly three pounds. The rainbow was kicking quite hard at this stage but the big one simply held on. Ten minutes later he was still doing so. I then lost sight of the encounter, presumably because the captor was by then sufficiently in control of the situation to take his catch to the bottom. So it looks as if the trout's technique is simply to wait until the victim is quite dead before attempting to pouch it.

As Richard Walker pointed out years ago, there is absolutely no doubt that a big trout is very happy to take a small fish even if it is already dead, a scavenging habit that some fishers may prefer to associate with pike and eels. My boys and I were pike-fishing on the Kennet one winter day, dead-baiting with sprats. Observing one of them in some kind of foul-up or tangle I put my sprat into a piece of slack water and left it to fish on its own while I went to the rescue. On my return ten minutes later I tightened up into something which went off with a most un-pike-like rush. It turned out to be a terrific brown trout of at least five pounds which by some miracle was hooked very cleanly in the mouth by just the lower of the two treble hooks. It went back in very good order, but though I returned to the spot several times during the following mayfly season, there was never a sign of it again.

References to the Misbourne start in 1925.

July 15th 1925

> "Went to Bob Lee's newly discovered pub at Little Missenden and had an astonishingly good evening. I killed nine fish, lost about twelve, and missed any number – best luck on the Alder and White Moth."

By the end of that season at Missenden Father had caught 162 trout and killed 57 averaging about ¾ lb. The best seems to have been a rainbow of about 1½ lbs., but there were very much bigger fish about in this tiny stream.

September 24th 1925

> "Netted Suffolk Bridge with the keeper and shifted a lot of fish including one of 4½ lbs. and two of 2¼ lb."

During 1925 Father was invited to fish as a guest on the Piscatorial Society's water on the Lambourn. The Misbourne took something of a back seat thereafter, although he certainly did not lose touch with it altogether.

May 20th 1936

> *"To Chorley Wood to buy 50 rainbows for John Brazil. Then to get rabbits for penned fox cubs at Amersham, but it was too cold – none out. John drove to the factory, killed three sheep in three minutes and gave the foxes the heads."*

Yet another little Buckinghamshire stream was simply called 'the Hambleden stream' and fell into the Thames near that village, just below the famous weir where Hobbs took many a Thames trout. Father probably got access to that by way of a windfall along with a small shoot which he and a few others rented at the time. Although the shoot was of only about 200 acres it was long, and narrow and situated in between two large estates, both of which reared a lot of pheasants. Not all of these stayed at home, and when they were added to the snipe and duck along the water meadows, a very useful shoot was the result. It's not quite true to say that the party rented the shoot because I believe in fact they paid nothing for it; the deal was that Father and a few others had to stay afterwards to play ha'penny nap with the farmer over a drink, or several drinks. Nobody got home very early.

Like the streams of Hertfordshire the little rivers (as they once were) of the Chilterns tend nowadays to be only shadows of their former selves in terms of the volume of water going down them. Presumably abstraction is at the bottom of it.

By the age of about thirteen I was distinctly frustrated where trout-fishing was concerned. My first couple of fish had, indeed, come to the net (of which more later) but there was no regular opportunity to fish for them. At the same time I lived in an atmosphere of trout-fishing. Father's friends would call and collect

81

him for a day out, and there would be the fish to admire in the sink when he got back. *The Fishing Gazette*, thin and with a green cover, was then about the only angling paper and regular reading of that stoked up my frustration. Most of the authors wrote under pen-names, and Father, in fact, put in one or two under the pseudonym 'South Bucks'. All seemed incredibly successful and such passages would occur as "I fished hard all the morning for only moderate results; six trout averaging a pound and two seatrout of 2 and 2½ pounds. However, after lunch, things began to look up . . ." and so on. It was all very hard to put up with.

Then, as now, *Where to Fish* was the bible of those seeking fishing, and I pored over it long and hard. The only piece of trout water that seemed geographically even remotely possible was the Chess. Here it was reported that the Duke of Bedford had two private stretches, one at Chenies and one at Sarratt. This Duke was, of course, the father of the one who so successfully built up Woburn as a tourist attraction.

I was moaning about all this to Father one day. In pursuit of his 'ask and it shall (perhaps) be given to you' principle, he said, "Well, why don't you just write and ask for permission to fish?"

After a lot of thought and a good many rough copies, the letter went off. "Your Grace, I am very keen on trout-fishing, etc. etc." To my own complete amazement, and I think Father's also, though of course he did not let on, a letter arrived a few days later, ducally crested (or so I imagine after forty odd years). It was from the Duke's agent, and contained a permit to fish either water. Now all that remained was to get there.

Some friends of my mother's owned an Austin 7 Ruby Saloon, and kindly rallied round to take me over to Chenies and drop me at the mill which stood at the lower end of the water. The river here was rather canalised and slow, but as I walked up it got more interesting, with little weirs just a foot high or so here and there. At the top I fitted up the Allcock Hexacane and set to work – downstream, with a Peter Ross.

It did not occur to me that perhaps the dry-fly would be more *comme-il-faut* on such a river. In any case, nothing was rising at that stage, and there was nothing on my ticket to say that dry-fly fishing was the rule. Subsequent meetings with the river-keeper brought no reprimand, and I've often wondered since whether everybody fished wet or dry as the circumstances demanded, or whether they were just being kind to a small boy. Anyway, off I went, and before long started to get a fish or two. None were of any great size until eventually a trout started to rise just upstream of one of the miniature weirs. Without changing the fly, an Invicta by this time, I covered the fish from below, having just enough sense to put the fly only inches above the fish so that the drag would have the least possible chance to start. He took it first chance and came tumbling back over the weir. Fortunately everything held, and he turned out to be 1½ lbs.

Moving on down to the canal-like stretch I learned a painful if simple lesson which has brought quite a few fish subsequently, although it's still all too easy to get it wrong in practice. There was no movement anywhere, and I was simply covering the water, moving a place or two down after each cast and retrieving the fly by a series of draws on the line. Suddenly, behind the fly, a wave started to develop as a trout came up to take. My nerve held until the final boil started to develop, at which point, (of course) I snatched the fly expertly from its jaws. It gave me a good view as it turned away, and was a real thumper. It was immediately apparent that I should have waited for the line to move, but nothing gave me a second chance.

All the same, the final bag was three takeable fish, duly recorded in a letter of thanks to a very kind benefactor. Subsequently I received another invitation, and this time went to Sarratt.

The difference this time was that the keeper appeared and accompanied me for part of the time in the role of ghillie, much against my wishes though I didn't dare say so. It was partly that fishing had by then become for me far more of a solitary than a convivial occupation, but probably more that I didn't want him to watch the bungling casting. As it turned out, he knew even less about the job than I did, and demonstrated this while we were having lunch.

Towards the lower end of the Sarratt stretch the river came to a dead end, and was turned sharply at a right-angle through a hatch-pool with vertical concreted sides.As we sat eating our sandwiches beside this pool, a fish became visible in the fast water, several feet down. I unshipped the fly, and while we ate, dangled it to and fro over the trout's head. After about five minutes, against all likelihood, it suddenly shot up and took the fly. The scene became animated, tomato sandwiches and ginger beer flying in all directions. The keeper seized the net. Then, as I fetched the fish in to the side, he grabbed the line in one hand, and with the other swung the net down in butterfly-catching fashion to trap the trout against the side of the pool. He then drew the net upwards, eventually trapping the fish in the pouch of the net. It was an astounding performance, and did my poor gut cast no good at all; it finished up well lacerated by the concrete and the point had to be replaced.

What a nuisance those gut-points were! Indeed, what a nuisance gut itself was. Modern anglers are spared the tedium of soaking their casts (or leaders) before any knot can be tied, and of having fairly regularly to replace the fine point. These were about eighteen inches long and were sold in the various strengths (3X, 4X and so on) in packets of half a dozen, from memory. Recently the father of a friend died and his tackle was passed on to me. He had not fished for some years, and it was nostalgic to find among the spools of nylon a soaking-box just such as we used to use. Father did at one time own the proper article, a round japanned tin with hinges so that both ends would open, giving two compartments presumably for casts and for points. Like much else of his gear it would no doubt be a collector's item now, if it had not all disappeared during the war and various post-war upheavals.

Despite their many deficiencies, Father's diaries provide some fascinating material, especially the oddities. His tales of the renowned Bisham pool, for example, cannot have been entirely fabulous, since on April 5th 1926 he caught a trout of 1 lb. 13 oz. there on minnow (just about sizeable by Thames standards, the size limit being then 16 inches).

In August 1926 we suddenly get three days recorded in Wales, on the river Gwendraeth. My brother Barry would then have been three years old and I a babe of eighteen months. This must have been another occasion when Father had been made to take a seaside holiday, salvaging an outing or two on some local stream. The results were not startling, seven fish for three outings at an average of 6 ounces. I can dimly remember a later visit to Wales, staying in a house and being well spoiled by various young Welsh girls who were rounded up to look after us. A photograph survives, showing Father standing in a no doubt ice-cold sea, holding Barry and me each by the hand, all grinning for the benefit of the Brownie box camera, all clad in decent one-piece, shoulder-to-thigh bathing costumes.

Chapter Six

When Father joined the Piscatorial Society in 1926, it was very probably at the suggestion of colleagues in the Royal Flying Corps, several of whose names crop up in his diaries.

One of the oldest fishing clubs in the world, the Piscatorial Society was founded in 1836 by a number of friends who used to meet at the Granby Tavern in South Audley Street, in London. The objectives were social as well as piscatorial, and all discussion of religion and politics was excluded.

The Society nowadays concerns itself almost exclusively with fly-fishing for trout and grayling, with a very heavy emphasis on the dry fly and small, Skues-type nymphs fished near the top; heavy nymphs only come into play for grayling in the autumn. There is not now even any lake fishing for trout, which was provided during the 1970s and early '80s. It has not always been like this. Until a few years ago the Chamberhouse water on the Kennet provided the relatively small number of members who were interested with the opportunity to catch good chub and barbel in the autumn and winter, with plenty of roach and dace as well. There were one or two who made excellent practice at trotting for grayling.

I once had a brown trout of about 6 lbs. on worm when trying for a barbel in October. Mattew, my eldest son, had an even bigger one on luncheon meat. Both these went safely back, and though we haunted the places during the mayfly, we never saw so much as a scale of them.

In its earlier days the Society was definitely for all rounders, probably none more celebrated than H.T. Sheringham. Father left me one of his books, the delightful *Fishing – its cause, treatment and cure* and Sheringham wrote others more instructive though equally pleasurable. Another of Father's fishing books, by Philip Geen, had the admirably explicit title *What I have seen while fishing and how I have caught my fish*. Sheringham was probably typical of the members of his day, and has written of carp, pike, bream, roach and tench as well as trout and grayling. *The Fisherman's Bedside Book*, compiled by 'B.B' contains several of his pieces, including an account of a dawn foray to a pre-baited swim which yields bream, roach and eventually a carp of seven or eight pounds. This comes from 'An Angler's Hours' and is so evocative that surely few fishermen could fail to be stirred even reading it for the ninth or the ninetieth time.

The Society has continued to produce many other writers, right up to the present day. Its extensive library of all kinds of works on fishing must by now be unique, and includes very detailed records of the history and activities of the Society itself.

To start with, most of the fishing was done on waters close to London, the Middlesex Colne for example. As time has passed, there has been a gradual movement westwards. In Father's day the Society's water included stretches of the Gade in Hertfordshire, the Lambourn in Berkshire and the Test in Hampshire, and at some earlier time the West Wycombe water had been rented. By the time I joined in 1975 the nearest water to London was on the Lambourn, and on the Kennet below Newbury. Now all that has also gone, and water is held on the Avon, Wylye and Itchen.

One of the more extraordinary incidents from Father's time with the Society took place on their water on the Test just above the town of Romsey. In those days it was at this point that the riparian owners began to wonder whether the salmon were a welcome addition to their trout fishing or a menace because of their competition with the trout, and in particular, it was thought, by their tendency to destroy the spawning redds by their own nuptial activities. Further upstream there was little doubt in the matter and any salmon showing its nose in the Stockbridge area was very likely to get itself shot.

The year was 1929 and Father was staying at the White Horse in Romsey with Rupert White for the mayfly. The article which he wrote for, I imagine, *The Fishing Gazette*, makes it plain that it was a frustrating foray. The fish were there in plenty, and big ones too, but the water had been neglected for some years before the Society took it on, and weed was a constant hazard. His description of the mass of fly, and the big trout lunging about, is enough to turn one green with envy. He was using IX gut, fairly heavy weaponry, yet was still broken by a fish whose weight even he would not estimate. Heavy weed can, of course, defeat almost any strength of line if a fish gets well wedged, but one cannot help wondering how things might have gone for him had he been armed with modern nylon which is so much stronger than gut for a given thickness.

On Sunday 25th May in the early morning he managed a decent fish of 3½ lbs., which took the pattern he favoured above all others, Barrett's Tar Brush. This was a spent dressing with black and white hair and he used it even when the duns were coming down on the grounds that a large, fat and presumably lazy fish would prefer to go for something that he knew was not suddenly going to take off. Somehow I've never managed to do much good with it, and my own current favourite is one tied by Matthew. This is made from deer hair and floats like a cork. One quality which nobody could deny it is visibility. Most of his tyings happen to be very light in colour and the general effect is – well, glaring. Fishing a carrier of the Avon one day I mounted one of these but after a few casts it seemed so incongruous that I took it off and put on something more subdued. An hour later, fishless, I went back to Matthew's pattern and immediately started to rise some trout.

Back at Romsey, Father had by later in the day found an enormous fish which he, this time for some reason, tackled with a winged fly, no doubt one of those curly duck-feather affairs which give me, at any rate, an immediate attack of no-confidence. The fish moved to him several times without ever properly taking hold. A council of war resolved that the fish was a salmon, and Rupert White set about it with a prawn on a single hook. This was taken but at the strike the hook failed to hold; the fish could be seen nosing about seeking the morsel which had been snatched from it, and in fact it took the broken prawn when it was thrown in again. This time it was hooked.

After the fish had been played for a while it became apparent that it was in fact a huge trout. When it came to the moment of landing Father, whose nerves must have been jangling like telephone wires by this time, managed to make a bosh shot with the gaff and succeeded only in scarring the fish's cheek. Someone else completed the job, and the party retired to celebrate at the White Horse.

The whole incident is described in the 1946 reprint of The Fisherman's Bedside Book by BB, though I think it disappeared in later editions. I have a copy of what Father described as a libellous photograph of the trout, which weighed 15 lb. 12 oz. It was taken with the trout lying on its stomach and certainly does not present an attractive view of what was apparently an extremely handsome fish, apart from a rather pronounced beak.

The Society also had water on the Lambourn, near Newbury. In the first full flush of his enthusiasm Father apparently fished it on twenty-three days during the April and May of 1926. How can he possibly have managed it? As far as I know he was not unemployed at the time, but it's true that his pay depended to quite an extent on commission so it was perhaps up to him how he organised his time – an agreeable situation.

More to the point, how did he get down there? Most of the dates are bracketed and are clearly week-ends, and in some cases these have been extended by a day, but this is by no means always the case. Newbury is today perhaps an hour's drive from High Wycombe. In those days, with more rudimentary roads but much less traffic it was probably about the same, but the fact was that Father did not then, and only once subsequently, own a car.

Public transport was a lot more comprehensive then, but the most likely answer is that he found, as he had a happy knack of doing, some compliant friend to drive him, perhaps combining this with stays in some small local pub. The White Horse at Romsey might have been affordable for the occasional Test trips but I cannot believe his finances would have run to regular stays at, say, the Chequers at Newbury, for the Lambourn fishing.

During the rest of the year his visiting-rate dropped off very sharply. After June 6th he went no more until July 18th (one trout 8 ounces) and thereafter five times for the rest of the year. Certainly a lot of people in those days felt that fly-fishing on chalk-streams was not particularly worth-while once the mayfly had finished. The Lambourn mayfly comes relatively early compared with the Kennet into which it falls. On one occasion I saw one drifting down on May

11th, and was only just in time at that, because within a yard, a trout had taken it. One of the great beauties of the Lambourn is that, small and clear as it is, the trout have the surface always under close supervision, and take up their opportunities smartly. It's not necessary to wait for a prolonged hatch to get them going, and indeed, if there is no surface fly at all, any fish that is up and on the fin and active is always open to the offer of a dry fly.

At the start of the season his fish averaged just under half a pound, but by the time May was well advanced, it was nearer three-quarters of a pound. This may have been due to the improvement in condition of the fish plus a little growth, or perhaps to his better ability, with experience, to pick out the heavier fish to cast to.

Grayling featured from time to time and, it would appear, were considered an undesirable feature of such a stream and killed. One good fish of 1¼ lbs. is recorded.

There are a few entries about the Lambourn fishing, which appears to have been at the very bottom end of the river at Newbury, just before it joins the Kennet.

April 26th 1925

> *"Fished Lambourn after breakfast. Fish rising freely between hailstorms. I missed them, also very freely. Met two very nice old men at the Swan, Dr. Drew and Mr Brown, who, though great friends, sat and rowed all night. Lost my train at Newbury, but got to Maidenhead and walked home."*

April 3rd 1926

> *"Returned 5 trout and killed a 1 lb. grayling on a fly spoon!"*

April 11th 1926

>*"Good hatch about mid-day. Hooked and rose more fish than I have ever done except during last year's mayfly. Killed 3, returned 9. Lost my scissors, oil-bottle and a lot of flies."*

July 24th 1926

>*"Went by car with Bob Lee to Burchett's Green, then caught the Greyhound bus to Newbury. No good at all in the daytime – caught one small fish on wet fly in the Dog Pool. Took a pup over for the Groves. Back by train in the evening, playing bridge and vingt-et un with some Oxford undergraduates."*

September 3oth 1926

>*"To Missenden and killed the last trout of the season, a small rainbow.*

Records for the year:

	Caught	Killed
Newbury	230	68
Missenden	72	32
Andover	3	2
Elsewhere	17	12
	322	114

Total weight 68 lbs. 10 oz. best 2 lbs. 2 oz.

Clearly the fish to be taken on both Misbourne and Lambourn were not enormous. This was long before the days when it became customary to stock even small streams with portly stew-fed fish.

In May 1928, Father received the following letter from either the Secretary or the President of the Piscatorial Society – the signature is illegible.

> Dear Pierce,
>
> The Committee have asked me to write and express their great appreciation and admiration of your action in rescuing the small boy from the Lambourn at Easter.
>
> Yours sincerely,
> ****************

Father's diary notes, of this incident:

April 7th 1928

> "Returned 3. Good rise in the morning which was, however, spoilt by a small boy falling in. I had to go in and fetch him out. Very cold."

I have certainly never caught as many fish as Father, but can at least equal him in small boys rescued. When pike-fishing on a Norfolk gravel pit with a friend there came a loud splash, soon revealed as being caused by his small son falling in. Like Father I 'had to go in and fetch him out', only discovering, as we floundered to the bank, that there was about fifteen feet of water under us. Both of us were well wrapped up and gumbooted, and I was glad enough to get out.

I myself joined the Piscatorial Society in 1975, remaining a member until 1982, after which I became involved in the management of some water nearer to home, and gave up membership. The fishing then still included a stretch of the Lambourn. It was always one of my favourites, a real little jewel of a stream. Though not large, the trout are very free-rising and because of the small scale on which everything is happening it's possible to see most of the action most of the time. It's very seldom that there is no surface activity at all, and in the spring hatches can be good enough to get the whole river going. Somehow the mayfly seems almost incongruous in this Lilliput, but they certainly take it well enough.

Next to the river there is a lake which the Society also rented and stocked with rainbows. This provided a most interesting supplement to the fishery, and my usual procedure in summer was to spend the day on the river and then move on to the lake for the last hour. This almost invariably produced a tremendous rise to chironomids or buzzers, which was by no means easy to deal with, and, to me at any rate, provided sport well up to the standard of the dry-fly fishing on the Lambourn, with the difference that the fish were anything up to four pounds or more instead of perhaps a pound (and very often not that). Reluctant as one is to concede the imported rainbow any virtue at all over the native brown, the genuine article as it were, it has to be admitted that they do provide an exciting fight and a rather better meal. Certainly Lambourn browns in particular have a reputation for low palatability.

The lake, which was fed directly from the river also contained some good brown trout. One night when for once there had been no general rise at all, I was returning to the boat house when just one fish started sipping away at the top end, where there was still a little current under the trees. Eventually I got the midge pupa to him correctly and he turned out to be a brown of over three pounds.

A week later a very similar situation arose. This time it was a 6 ounce grayling.

Father's lack of a car was probably partly financial but also unquestionably due to the fact that he was almost totally without mechanical ability. This might seem strange in one who in his flying days had mastered the not-inconsiderable intricacies of the Lewis machine-gun, but of course the incentive to get it right must then have been much greater than when, for example, mending the mower. Any watch he wore or carried seemed to stop within a matter of days, and the chain which spanned his middle when I first dimly remember him carried only an ivory elephant, on one end, and on the other the bullet which had been dug out of his thigh in 1917. All the same, this characteristic of mechanical inability probably owed a lot also to the fact that he did not believe in keeping a dog and barking himself. With a wife and two boys about the place, why get mixed up with such tedious matters? He even used to ask one of us to turn on the wireless.

Immediately after the 1914-1918 war he had briefly ventured into the world of motor-cycling. It had not been a success. Many of the motor-bikes in those days had no kick-start – the engine was stimulated into action by the bump-start technique. The rider ran along, pushing the machine, which was in gear but with the clutch out. When sufficient speed was attained the clutch was let out, the engine fired, and the rider leaped nimbly into the saddle. Father's machine, variously described as an Indian and an Enfield, was a sulky starter. On more than one occasion, when it finally roared into life, Father was too exhausted to execute the necessary leap, and finished in a heap in the gutter.

His nephew George, son of a much older brother, used to be recruited to clean the bike, in return for an occasional pillion ride. They were once sailing together up the very steep Amersham hill, which leads out of the centre of High Wycombe, when they were assailed by an enormous dog. Father was suddenly surprised by an unexpected extra turn of speed up the hill, caused when the dog seized poor George and dragged him off the pillion.

During the subsequent war I found myself for a time in charge of motor-cycle instruction, and once took the whole squad over to meet Father who happened to be in the district. We put him up on the sergeant-instructor's pillion (which for some reason he preferred to mine) and we had an agreeable foray over the moors. When we stopped by a small stream for a smoke, a milk bottle could be seen on the stream bed. I explained to the recruits, all town men, that a small trout might take shelter by such a handy piece of cover. One of them stepped into the water in his riding boots and picked the bottle up; there was a little trout actually inside it. It was difficult to tell whether Father or the recruits were more impressed.

Unfortunately my reputation as the knowledgeable countryman took a severe blow a few days later. Once again we were having a short break, when a sheep appeared on a steep crag above us. I was just explaining about the sure-footedness of these creatures when it missed its footing and fell heavily down the rock face.

Father did once own a motor-car, if only briefly. It was bought for one specific purpose, to enable him to bring about the downfall of an enormous brown trout which he had located not in the Kennet itself but in the nearby Kennet and Avon canal at Thatcham in Berkshire. Clearly the mayfly would provide the opportunity and so the car was bought, and a series of friends laid on to drive it down

97

each evening. Some work must have set in at this time or he would probably have been camping down there.

My own mechanical knowledge is on a par with his (although I did once have an engineering triumph on a farm, getting a broken-down corn drill back into action by use of a well-placed nail) and no memory remains of make or type. It was always referred to as the barouche; irretrievably open, it had a good deal of brass where nowadays would be tinny chrome. The doors only came part of the way down the body, their handles rather elegant little brass loops.

Evening after evening the expedition would set out, to trail back disconsolate after nightfall. He never did catch that fish and when the mayfly season ended, the barouche was put into the garage, which generally lay empty. My brother and I and a couple of friends once laboriously pushed it back up the sloping drive and then Barry took the wheel and we let it roll away. For one glorious moment I thought he was going to go straight through the back of the garage, but he managed to pull up with only a slight jolt to the bumper, of which the strength and construction was such that there was barely a mark. Not that Father would have noticed.

People took to borrowing the barouche. At first, permission would be asked, but after a time the garage would simply be empty, with a note on the door saying, perhaps 'Have taken the barouche – 2nd XI is playing away' or something of the sort. Eventually it simply disappeared, and that was the last time any member of our immediate family owned a motor until 1952. I was managing a farm, and on a loan from my employer bought an ancient Hillman with a soft top. Father saw it once, not long before he died, and after a few moments' study, commented carefully.

"That doesn't look to me like a very good car." It wasn't. Before very long it was a starting-handle job every time. It also suffered a very curious accident. At that time I played cricket for the village of Kingston Deverill in Wiltshire, and we parked our cars in the cricket field. Unfortunately the field also contaianed a couple of horses, which while we were all distracted with the game, called round to browse on my car roof. The canvas was in sections, with piping, and presumably they bared their nasty yellow teeth, took hold of the piping and simply peeled the thing like an orange. I mended it with the Copydex which was normally used to repair combine sacks, but it was never quite the same.

Chapter Seven

Father's attack on the Thatcham trout took place somewhere about 1935, when I was ten. Around that time he also started to take me with him sometimes to watch him fish for salmon on the Test. This was on the Broadlands water below Romsey. At that time, day-tickets could be obtained, and after a period when I think only season rods were available, this is once again the case.

In those days there was a small run of big fish in the early spring, followed by a much more plentiful supply of smaller fish in the summer. Tickets were cheaper in the spring and autumn, and that's when Father mostly used to go. His diary records anything from one to seven visits in the course of a year.

He kicked off with a fish of 10 lbs. 8 oz. on prawn on September 25th 1927, apparently on only his second day's salmon fishing ever. The diary reports:

September 25th 1927

> *"Water fined down, but not so much as hoped. Missed three fish, and landed one of just under 11 lbs. Had a rare job to get White to come and gaff it. While he was coming, he caught his fly in the backside of his trousers. Lost a fish for an old man through not understanding the blowing of a whistle. Nearly ran over a fox on the way home."*

The following year two visits in August produced a fish each at 14

14 lbs. and 11 lbs., the latter very unusually on fly, Thunder and Lightning. The water at Broadlands is in most places deep and powerful, and the majority of fish were taken on prawn or Devon minnow or some other spun lure. In 1930 came his first big fish, one of 27 lbs. 8 oz. on eel-tail.

1935 seems to have been the best season. Six visits are recorded for a total of nine fish. Three of these (13 lbs., 12 lbs. 8 oz., 12 lbs.) came on April 14th, all to prawn. This, I think, cannot have been the occasion when he took three in a day with his right forearm in plaster, the result of not accurately judging one of the brisker deliveries from High Wycombe's star fast bowler. I was there on that occasion with Barry, and distinctly remember that as we came home with the fish it was a warm and balmy summer night.

Our chauffeur was Boo Pearce, no relation, who owned a bull-nose Morris car with a dickey-seat, or in American parlance, rumble-seat. When this was open, there remained a more or less flat ledge behind the saloon part of the car, and it was here that the three fish were loaded. Barry and I had to keep re-stowing them. Celebratory stops were quite frequent, and eventually we were halted by a policeman. As soon as he saw the fish all interest in any possible motoring offence was forgotten, and Father had to give a blow-by-blow account. We trundled on through Marlow and home. Overhead the bats were hawking to and fro after moths. Those of us in the dickey-seat had drunk no more than ginger beer, but the excitement, the speed, and the warm night air combined to generate a magical, light-headed feeling as we rumbled past Whincup's Meadow and down Marlow Hill into High Wycombe.

Father's best salmon at Broadlands, or anywhere else for that matter, was one of 31 lbs. in March 1936, and I was there to see it. It was on No. 1 Beat, which followed the upstream beat called The Rookery, and led off into Numbers 2 and 3. No. 1 was unquestionably his favourite. At the top end was a fishing hut which served both Rookery and No. 1. Here also was a weed-rack, and a cut to a hatch-pool feeding a substantial carrier. The carrier went off across the water meadows and fell into the main river again lower down. From the weed-rack there was a deep, powerful stretch which would have been rather featureless had it not been for the construction of a number of short wooden groynes which had been put there not for any kind of water-engineering but simply to provide lies for the salmon. Then came the pool supreme, Black Dog, and this is where the 31-pounder was landed, after being hooked in Long Reach, just upstream.

This time, a Devon minnow did the trick, fished with the heavy split-cane rod and Nottingham reel. My principal memory of the affair is of the line actually hissing through the water when the fish made a run. Father's policy at all times was to get a fish on the bank in the shortest possible time. This was possibly not so much for humanitarian reasons, though these are undoubted, but more in the belief that the longer a fish is in play, the more chance there is that it will find a snag or that the hook-hold will give way. Provided that all the gear is sound this seems like very good sense, and I remember horrifying one of the more staid members of the Piscatorial Society during the mayfly on the Kennet by bundling out a trout of about 1½ lbs. a few seconds after hooking it. With a 6 lbs. b.s. leader and a water with plenty of weed, it seemed a reasonable approach.

As Father piled the pressure on to his fish, I was despatched at a run to the next fishing hut at the foot of the beat, to fetch the redoubtable Walter Geary, head keeper at Broadlands. But before I got there he emerged with the gaff, and came up the bank at a brisk walk – no running for him. The gaffing was a first-shot affair, and then we were all admiring this really magnificent fish. The lilac sheen on the silver of a fresh-run and freshly-caught salmon is something unique, and in reproduction is seen only in the very best of photographs. I don't think I've ever seen a painting which does it justice.

Then it was back to the fishing hut, where the fish was laid out in the cool. The Broadlands huts were substantially built in wood and surrounded with a stout fence to keep the cattle off. The interiors of all had a highly characteristic smell of fish and formalin, the latter from the many jars of bottled sprats which had been opened and, no doubt, spilled there over the years. For some reason Father never used the dyed golden sprat which was favoured by many of the rods, preferring the Devon minnow or, above all, the prawn. On the wall of this hut was a copy of the famous H. M. Bateman cartoon, 'The man who used an Alexandra on the Test.' Although this is a good enough fly it has never, for me at any rate, produced the enormous number of huge trout shown as caught by the gleeful angler in this cartoon. On the bank, retired colonels and tweeded keepers fainted or burst with apoplexy at the shock of this villain using such a fly in the Test, sacred to the dry fly. The joke, in fact, however applicable to the upper reaches at Leckford or Whitchurch, had little relevance at Broadlands where the trout were very much an incidental, seldom fished for except in the mayfly and the grannom.

I caught my first trout on the fly on No. 1 Beat at Broadlands (not on an Alexandra). The arrangement was that salmon fishers could fish for trout also for 5/- (about 25p) per day. I only remember Father taking this up on two occasions apart from my own venture.

The first time there was a good hatch of grannom and he took a nice fish from the carrier which left the main river just above the bottom of No. 2 Beat. The fish was rising steadily in the calm water above a set of hatches. This was the first time that I had ever been able to see a fish quite clearly as it lay in position to feed and the excitement was intense as our fly floated down, to be taken with perfect confidence. It was not a large fish by Test standards, about 1¾ lbs., but played a large part in hooking me forever on fly-fishing. It has probably also been responsible for my putting down many a subsequent fish. I can never resist trying to put myself into a position from which the quarry can be watched while it's attacked, and this sometimes proves to be fatally too close. All the same I do believe that in the long run you get more fish by crawling as close as you can, for the best possible observation, than you do by adopting the 'fine and far off' approach which so often results in a miss on the strike.

The other occasion when Father invested five shillings in the trout-fishing was during one mayfly season. The Broadlands water, relatively slow and deep was not an ideal trout water, but those it held ran to very heavy weights. These big fish rarely showed except in the mayfly, and at this time they made an exceptionally good five shillings worth for anyone who would tear himself away from the possibility, however remote, of a thirty-pound salmon. On this particular occasion the hatch was extremely sparse and Father spent very little time with the trout. He did not in fact score, but I remember the day for an excellent demonstration of the value of accurate marking of a rise.

As small boys do, I had gone mooning off on some private investigation. When I got back to Father he was just changing back to a salmon rod.

"A good fish took one mayfly about two-thirds of the way between here and that big clump of reeds," he said. "Keep an eye on the spot and when I come back, tell me whether he's been feeding."

This was on the featureless stretch between Black Dog and the weed-rack. I sat there for an hour, and never saw a movement to any of the occasional flies which drifted down. Father then arrived back and hearing my report, decided he would have a couple of casts anyway. The first one fell. "Too short," he commented. He lengthened the line, and the fly settled; immediately a large neb appeared and down went the fly. When Father tightened up the fish simply took off and slammed into a large bed of weed. That was that, but it did not detract from a virtuoso performance of accurate marking.

My own foray on No. 1 Beat took me to a stretch of broken water between Black Dog and the Oak Tree pool, the idea being that this would disguise the heavy fall of fly and leader resulting from very ham-fisted casting. It didn't take long to find a rising fish and soon I was thrashing away with some sort of Olive on the end. Eventually the fish made a mistake and out it came – a trout of about ¾ lb. On the Test this of course is a mere minnow, but nothing was going to stop me showing this triumph to Father and in any case nobody had actually mentioned a size limit. The trout got a sharp crack on the head from the net handle. I turned to find Walter Geary standing behind me.

"Can I keep it?" I stammered.

"It looks as if you'd better," he replied, grinning through the pipe which was almost perpetually clamped between his teeth.

Walter Geary was in charge of the Broadlands fishing for many years. I never saw him fish the fly but he was certainly an artist with spinning tackle. Just above the fishing hut at the bottom of No. 2 Beat the far bank was for about thirty yards made firm by camp-sheathing, a stretch of stout wooden planking. This produced a steady run which often held a fish. The river narrowed by about five down its length. We watched Walter Geary fish down this one day with a prawn, taking a stride between each cast. Every single time the prawn dropped in no more than six inches out from the boards.

He told us one day of an extremely ingenious if villainous method of taking a salmon during the hottest days of summer when salmon tended to lie, inert and log-like, interested in nothing. In these conditions, he said, they would not move to any fly or bait, and seemed indifferent even to the presence of a fisherman close to them. A mere poacher would simply gaff or stroke-haul them with a heavily weighted set of trebles, the 'Walkerburn Angel' which we're told is still in common use in Scotland and Wales. This would hardly do for even the most unscrupulous rod who had taken a beat on the Test. However, if one were to mount a very large salmon fly (a strange choice, perhaps, in the weather conditions, but who's to judge for sure what a salmon will take and when?), and if one were then to reel this tight up against the top ring, there would be a rather useful gaff, and barbed at that. The gape of the hook would be smaller than that of your average gaff, but on the other hand, the reach would be a great deal longer. The final subtlety was that a skilled practitioner could set the hook at least on the outside of the jaw, while the real artist would place it actually inside the mouth (presumably while the fish was yawning). Once hooked, the fish would be played in the normal way, and the keeper arriving hot foot with the conventional gaff would be none the wiser. If he felt that a Jock Scott four inches long was a strange fly on which to take a fish from a low river in mid-August, why, that would be his privilege.

Here are some of the diary entries about his Test fishing; most of these relate to Broadlands, some to the Piscatorial Society water:

February 18th & 19th 1928

> "*A very nice weekend at Romsey. Water high, meadows flooded, and I don't think any fresh fish were up. Caught 2 kelts. Had several prawns smashed up. Sir George Richardson, aged 81, had a party at the White Horse for his wedding – he was a gay old bird. The father-in-law had an ear trumpet. Tattersall came down and left me a bottle of Crofts 1912 port, which was very good.*"

February 25th 1928

> "*To Romsey with Hammond and Dove. We each caught a kelt. Mine was a very large, well-rounded fish and I didn't like returning him. He shook his head and drove the hook well into my thumb. Very amusing to watch a plover mobbing a redshank, which lay flat in the water when attacked.*"

September 16th 1928

> "*Romsey with Jack Gibson and Nicholas after playing a tie at Reading on a poisonous wicket. Pretty well everyone was hit, and I had to stand back. No luck at all at Romsey – brilliant weather and water like glass.*"

October 14th 1928

> "*A wonderful day at Romsey. I had two – 17 lbs. (fly) 10 lbs. (spinning prawn). White had two – 14 lbs. and 15 lbs. Marjorie White one – 11 lbs. Edge two – 18 lbs. and 12½ lbs. I was broken twice and Edge missed gaffing a big fish for me.*"

February 22nd 1929

> *"An astonishing start at Romsey. I was not very well (Old Contemptibles Dinner overnight) but landed a beautiful 27½ lbs. fish from Cowman's Pool after 40 minutes. He took an eel tail. Dove was sure it was a kelt, and I did all sorts of things, letting Lionel Parker hold the rod, and even giving the fish loose line."*

June 1st 1930

> *"A terrible, disastrous day at Romsey. Hooked one from the top bridge and he bolted under the weed-rack faster than any fish I have ever handled. After nearly breaking my rod he straightened out the hook. Geary immediately hooked another on my rod, which got off after we had, by a feat of gymnastics, passed the rod round the spikes."*

May 16th 1931

> *"Floating weed spoilt all the fishing. I caught a pike, spinning, where the salmon is. It gave me quite a thrill for a moment, but we could soon see what it was. It had four lampreys inside it."*

September 27th 1931

> *" . . . Hooked another fish in the run below the Island Pool and thought I had a 40 lbs. fish. He went mad and got to Webb's Pool, where we kept him by stoning. Geary gaffed him very well, and we found he was hooked near the tail – a red cock fish of 18lbs.*

April 3rd 1932

> *"No. 1 Beat. Lost a fish in Kendle's Corner after trying him with all sorts of things. He came unstuck after taking a prawn.*

Another large fish, probably a trout, collared my lead."

March 26th 1933

"Romsey with Rupert White. Caught two or three kelts, but no fish. Hooked the bottom just before lunch – Rupert pulled it out from the opposite bank and hooked a kelt by hand on the way back. Refused to swop beats with Joe Davis at midday – Geary then caught him one of 32 lbs., and Shepherd one of 21 lbs."

April 5th 1936

"Last thing at night, put the prawn under the bridge at the bottom of No. 1, and almost at once hooked a fish. Handed the rod to Geary while I walked off the bridge, then walked him up to the pool. Eventually gaffed on the Platform – 28lbs."

March 20th 1937

"Hooked a fish under the bridge (No. 1 Beat) and, after much trouble got him – 21 lbs. Roger mounted the prawn which this fish took. Missed another fish that Roger had spotted under the opposite bank at the Oak Tree Pool."

March 20th 1937

"Rupert hooked a fish from the other bank and could not follow it down past the trees. I put my minnow over his line, hauled in, cut his line and re-tied it to mine. The fish went downstream and was eventually gaffed – 20 lbs."

Chapter Eight

The salmon of the Test were rightly regarded as being quite unsuitable for small boys to practice on. I went along with Father a good deal more frequently than did Barry, especially after he went away to school at thirteen or so. He preferred shooting and sailing in any case. My role was to carry the bag, run back to the hut to fetch anything which had been forgotten, raise the alarm when a fish was hooked and generally to make myself useful. While all this was in train, I could look, listen, and with a bit of luck, learn. One of the more interesting techniques to be studied was the extraction of salmon from beneath the several bridges which spanned the Broadlands water.

These were solidly based on two sets of stout timber piles sunk into the river bed. Thus there were three 'arches'. The salmon loved to lie against the uprights, and getting them out was liable to be even more difficult than hooking them in the first place. The whole situation held an irresistible fascination for Father, and once again his favourite lure was the prawn, nearly always mounted to be fished sink-and-draw, rather than spinning.

The procedure was to stand on the bottom rail of the wooden fence on the upstream side of the bridge. The prawn would first be dangled enticingly to and fro, up and down, in the area immediately below the leading edge of the bridge. If this brought no response it was necessary to lean further out and pay out more line, until the whole of the water under the bridge had been covered and the fisherman stood down, rather purple in the face by this time, since he had to bend well over to reach the last objective.

When a fish took hold, the great thing was not to bustle it too much. There was always a good chance that it would come quietly, and go upstream. If it could be persuaded to do this, Father would then tip-toe round the end of the bridge and revert to his normal hard-playing tactics in the clear water above. Not all salmon took this co-operative attitude; some clearly felt that this was the time to return to the ocean, and set off downstream with Father doubled up on the fence and the reel rattling, an enlivening scene.

There was a drill for this eventuality. Even the most strong-willed fish would generally settle into some resting lie if no great pressure were applied to it. Once this situation was established an assistant, be he boy or keeper (and on one great occasion I did it), would gaff up the line from the downstream side of the bridge. Loose line was paid off from the reel, and the line then cut. Father would then tear across to the downstream side, knot the line together again, easy enough with the stout flax line then in use, and after barely taking up the pressure again on the fish, he would walk down the bank, shortening the line all the time. Once he was below the fish the odds were well in his favour.

As far as I recall, no fish ever moved off during the crucial few seconds when it was being, as it were, hand-lined, but it was always an exciting prospect. Presumably the hand-liner's duty would have been simply to hang on, at whatever risk to his fingers, or possibly to hurl himself into the river. Another interesting possibility was that a salmon would set off downstream and then immediately come back through a different arch. Father never recounted this as happening, but certainly on one occasion after the line-cutting operation had been completed, the fish ran back through the bridge again, and everything had to be repeated.

The landing of the heavy spring fish could very often be a tricky business. I was only about eleven when Father hooked a fish of about 25 lb. at the bottom of No. 2 Beat. It took him down almost to the bridge, where a kind of stalemate set in. The fish lay in a strong current right under the bank and about three feet down. A few more yards would have taken it through the bridge, but it simply hung there, and certainly nothing would induce it to come back up. I had scrambled down the awkward bank to report its position, and could have reached it with the gaff. Father, however, judged that what would have been a reasonable operation for Walter Geary would in my case be more likely to end up with my joining the fish rather than vice-versa. While he was nerving himself to hand me the rod and have a go himself, the hook straightened out. Words would probably have failed most people.

In that authoritarian age, fathers generally organised matters and small boys did what they were told, but I remember Broadlands as the scene of the first occasion when we 'did it my way', rather than Father's. We were at the top end of No. 3 Beat, about a couple of hundred yards downstream from the bridge, scene of the hook-straightening incident, where there was also a fishing hut. I was about twelve, and Father allowed me to have a few casts, something which happened extremely seldom. We had on a silver Devon minnow, and I plugged away with this for about five minutes, enjoying simply the action of casting. I don't think it crossed my mind that anything would take. Suddenly there was a solid thump, and I was in business. I had always noticed that whenever Father hooked a fish, a salmon at least, all the colour would drain from his face and he finished up as pale as a sheet; no doubt he was now observing the same phenomenon. He kept up an encouraging commentary as long as possible but eventually it became clear that this was a kelt. The net kept against this eventuality was of course back at the hut, and no keeper was in earshot.

"Shall I take the rod while you run back for the net?" said Father. It wasn't really a question.

"No – I'll hang on to the rod while you run back for the net – please."

And he did.

'Walking up' was one of the techniques for dealing with a fish which had got itself into an awkward downstream position. It's difficult to understand why it worked, but it certainly seemed to. Instead of remaining in one position and trying to 'pump' the fish back to recover line, the fisherman would clamp down on the reel and, with the rod well up, walk very slowly backwards up the bank. For some reason the fish would very often respond to this by allowing itself to be drawn along like a rather reluctant dog on a lead. The essence of the operation was perhaps its steadiness and the lack of any vibration from the reel.

Father let me have a go at this once with a large kelt at the very bottom end of the water, on No. 3 Beat. In the strong current it was extremely hard work indeed; it didn't occur to me until afterwards that this golden opportunity to gain further experience probably came to me only thanks to the fact that Father saw no reason to break his own back on the job when mine was available. In fact he had to take over in the end because I simply had not the strength to beat the fish.

Another job for boys was to run to the sound of any heavy

splash and mark where the fish had moved. One day Father was at work with his prawn when there was a dramatic aquatic commotion in the Oak Tree pool upstream – to call it a splash would be an understatement. I shot off to do my duty only to find that this had been caused by a cow falling in. She had obviously chosen the wrong place to take a drink, and the bank had collapsed beneath her.

A stout Shorthorn, she clearly found the amphibious life very little to her taste. Eyes rolling wildly, she was striking out strongly, so strongly in fact that she was holding her position against the current, not getting anywhere but not losing ground, (or water), either. It was all rather reminiscent of those scenes from Westerns when the herd fords the river on its way to Laramie. Except, of course, that this one was on her own.

I hurried back to make my report. This was just the sort of daft scenario that appealed to Father. Clearly the cow must be rescued, not just for humanitarian reasons, if that's the word, but also because the presence of this substantial ruminant bobbing about in a salmon pool could not be tolerated. The problem was, how to achieve it, bearing in mind that she probably weighed half a ton, albeit buoyed up by the water. I think Father quite fancied himself stripping off and going in to manhandle her to the bank. Commonsense for once prevailed, aided by the fact that it was a none-too-tropical spring day. The eventual method was to bombard the water round the cow's head with heavy clods. As each splashed violently in she flinched and gave way a bit, dropping a little downstream. Before long she grounded on the gravel at the tail of the pool and staggered ashore. No doubt as she tired this would all have come about without our assistance. We enjoyed it anyway.

On one occasion, though unfortunately I wasn't there to see it,

Father did strip off and go in, but this time with the far greater incentive of freeing a salmon which was hung up on weed or some snag in Black Dog. Walter Geary was present but quite rightly felt that it was no part of a head keeper's duty to take issue with a salmon in its own element. If an under keeper had been present, that might have been different. As it was, he took the rod and Father undertook the sub-aqua role. They got the fish in the end.

Although the main river was not an easy place in which to locate a trout, the carriers were a different proposition. The original function of most of these was to provide an aid to the management of the water meadows. The main carriers were like little rivers in their own right, perhaps seven or eight yards across. From these, smaller streams and runnels were taken, the whole system being controlled by sluices, the levels of which were remarkably precisely organised. Presiding over all this, and over many similar systems throughout the southern chalk stream areas, were some highly skilled 'drowners', now I think an extinct race. Their job in early spring was to operate the sluices so as to cover the meadows with a thin, and slowly moving, film of water. There may have been some benefit from the deposition of silt, but the principal result was to keep the soil a few degrees warmer by preventing frost getting in. This eventually meant an earlier flush of grass and a few very valuable extra weeks of grazing. Presumably for most of the rest of the year the drowners would be busy maintaining the channels and sluices.

These carriers held some splendid trout, with the great advantage that you could in fact spot them. Apart from Father's effort during the grannom I don't remember anyone fishing for them. No doubt they are nowadays being well exploited.

The carrier which left the river near the boundary between

Rookery Beat and No. 1 had a good hatchpool at the top end. It was here that I first realised how sadly one can be misled by the rises of a trout which is cruising, and came to understand the value of getting close enough to see what is really going on. The banks of this pool were well overhung with bushes, and at some cost in lacerated flesh it was possible to crawl forward and observe the water at close range. I had been watching the pool from below one day, seeing a number of rises in the steadier water at either side of the pool. It would have been easy to think that there were quite a few fish feeding. Then I crawled up to the edge, to find that the situation was quite otherwise.

All the rises were being made by just one trout, a handsome butter-yellow fish of about 2½ lbs. Not a care in the world, he sauntered along under one bank, picking up a beetle here or a caterpillar there. Then he crossed over at the bottom, and repeated the process up the other side. When he reached the fast water at the neck he slid through and carried on the process. He looked an absolute sitter, just asking for something like a Coch-y-bondhu to be hung out over the water and dibbled over his nose on the next circuit. But there was no trout-fishing that day.

On another occasion in the same pool Barry and I in collaboration attempted a dastardly deed which, perhaps fortunately, did not come off. The hatches which controlled the flow of water into this pool were very well oiled and maintained, and we found that we could easily wind them up and down. Playing with water is always highly enjoyable, and this time there was an added excitement. I was lying on my stomach looking down to where the concreted tunnel from the hatches led into the pool. Barry elected to cut the water off altogether, for a short while. As the level in the tunnel dropped to a a perilous few inches, a good trout which had been lying up there came shooting out into the pool.

After a council of war we restored the flow to normal, then lay in concealment to watch. After a long wait, the trout reappeared and went back up the tunnel. Barry went to the fishing hut where fortunately nobody was about, and came back with a landing net. Then, as I lay head down with the net over the route which the trout had taken, Barry once more cut off the water. The fish came charging out, but dodged the net without much difficulty. We tried the whole operation again with the same result; I felt rather like the wretched goal-keeper facing a penalty kick, almost bound to opt for the wrong line of attack. Given even a couple of yards of strawberry netting we would have had him.

Another combined operation had a more positive, if terrifying result. I cannot think that I'm alone in feeling that the best place for an eel is either in the river, or on a plate. It is impossible not to respect a fish whose migratory saga matches that of a salmon, and it is fascinating to see them prospecting about the bottom after food. They fight hard and are thoroughly worthy opponents. But once they are on the bank, the writhing, the slime, the tenacity, the beady little eye, all add up to pure horror. They are, in a word, sinister. It is of course absurd to look at any fish in this anthropomorphic way, yet by contrast with the eel, who could possibly kill, or feel anything but affection for a barbel? In 1984, after some fifty years of fishing, admittedly mostly for trout, I caught my first barbel, at about a pound in weight probably one of the smallest ever recorded on rod and line. With his blunt whiskery face, even at his tender age, he looked like somebody's favourite uncle, to be treated with affection. Indeed, I do not suggest an eel should be handled otherwise, but fishing is not all logic and I just don't like them. It seems likely that some fish feel the same. Matthew and I were one day on the bridge over the Border Esk at Potholme, above Langholm. Immediately below there is an expanse of clean gravel where the water settles down after a fast run just above the bridge, and against the left hand bank a large boulder. We had been watching a sea-trout of about 1½ lbs., which eventually took cover under the boulder, and also a foraging eel of certainly no more than ¾ lb. The eel nosed about, working his way across the stream, and finally insinuated himself under the boulder. Immediately, not only the first sea trout but another as well shot out and took up positions on the gravel a couple of yards away. They apparently were not prepared to share quarters with the eel, and I don't blame them.

Our horrific encounter with a Test eel took place on No. 3 Beat. Whether or not the records would bear this out, No. 3 was always regarded as last but one as a producer of salmon, after No. 1 and No. 2, in that order, but above Rookery. It was, however, a very attractive piece of water, including some shallower holes with a bottom of fine yellow sand. These gave excellent observation and there was one where a shoal of really superb roach could be seen drifting about in an eddy. In another much smaller pot-hole, Barry and I one day discovered a hefty eel.

It was an extremely hot August day. Father had gone off to fish the bottom end, leaving us stretched out on the grass by the lunch bag and most of the tackle. Sun-bathing soon palled, and it was when poking about the river bank that we came upon the eel. Like the one at Potholme years later it was clearly foraging and likely to be open to an offer, but of what? Traditionally in our eyes the bait for an eel would be a worm, but in such weather any sensible lobworm would

119

clearly be dozing several feet down. The day's menu, however, included ham sandwiches. Somehow we rigged up a crude hand-line with a prawn-hook on the end, impaled a chunk of ham and lowered it to our customer. After a brief inspection he pouched it, but it turned out to be we who had bitten off more than we could chew. Richard Walker has pronounced, how rightly, that there is no place for finesse in playing big eels, and in this case we only had a yard or two of line to play with. A joint heave, and the eel was on the bank, as fresh as a daisy and full of fight. Boys are not the most forward-thinking of creatures; we had concentrated so hard on getting the brute out that we had no plans whatever for dealing with him once he joined us on dry land. Practised eel-fishers no doubt approach the problem the other way round. After a desperate, sordid and (once again, illogically) frightening struggle we reached a silent but unmistakable understanding. Out came a pocket-knife, and soon the eel was back in its pool, wondering what all that was about. We returned to base.

Shortly afterwards Father also returned.

"I saw a rather good eel here earlier on," he said. "If you see it, you can have a go if you like."

We said we wouldn't bother.

Since then I've had a number of encounters with eels, and could have done without most of them. Fishing on the Border Esk for sea-trout at night, both Matthew and I had the disagreeable experience of hooking an eel on the fly. Mine was foul-hooked, but his had taken the fly properly. It is quite tricky landing and dealing with a sea-trout in the pitch dark, but a half-pound eel is in a class of its own.

It seemed very surprising at first that such encounters could occur, but fishing as we were with sink-tip lines, and bringing the flies in over the shallows at the end of the cast, it is in fact reasonable enough, bearing in mind the tendency of eels to come right into the shallow water at night. The faint plopping noises to be heard at the water's edge had always puzzled me when night-fishing, but Matthew eventually got to work with his torch and discovered that the noise was made by eels, presumably trying to collect some of the small fry which shoal close in.

Speaking of fry recalls another occasion on the Test which demonstrated that country people are not always the mine of information on natural history that one might sentimentally like to suppose. I've been fortunate enough to live most of my life in the country and have found that the fact is that a lot of countrymen are hardly interested in 'nature' at all, except so far as it affects their farming and gardening. We were shooting once and picked up a dead green woodpecker, (not shot, let it be said). The first man we showed it to in the pub at lunch-time thought it was a parrot.

I was by the Test one day in the company of one of the under-keepers, and was very interested in a shoal of fry which hung in a patch of quiet water behind some reeds. They were only an inch or two long and, to me, unidentifiable. It somehow did not seem likely that they were salmon; trout perhaps. I put the question to the expert.

"What are those, down there?"

The keeper bent down, studied the creatures for a few moments, and then made his pronouncement.

"Hinsecks."

The best view I've ever had of eels was shortly after what to people of my generation will always be 'the war'. It was 1947, and Marcel Winter-Taylor and I went over to Ireland to fish, and, as we hoped, to get some decent food. In neither of these objectives were

121

we wholly successful.

Certainly, as far as food was concerned, there was no scarcity of truly excellent raw materials. Ham, eggs, butter, cream and lots of other good things which neither of us had seen for years were plentiful. The drawback was in the cooking. We were not, of course, staying in any but the cheapest hotels, but even so, we felt that whoever was doing the cooking might from time to time have deployed something other than the frying-pan. The first plateful of fried ham and eggs was a real luxury. By the time we were getting back on the boat at Dun Laoghaire we were almost ready for another Woolton pie (for the younger reader, a ration-saving delicacy promoted by the then Minister of Food, Lord Woolton, and consisting largely of carrots). No doubt Irish cuisine is very different now.

The fishing was rather mixed too. It had not then dawned on me that when one sets off to fish a new area, accurate intelligence is almost more vital than the rod itself. Purely on the suggestion of an Irish friend, we set off to Mrs — 's Fishing Hotel, not so very far from Dublin, in Co. Wicklow. There was a fine lough by the hotel, and at that stage of our fishing knowledge, the dark peatiness of its water conveyed nothing. For the first two days we kept catching and returning trout which ran at about three to the pound, before we eventually met a local fisherman and discovered that that was the average weight for the lough. The only way to get a bigger fish was by trolling. We tried this for a day and found it deadly boring (in other words, we didn't get one).

It was at Galway that we saw the mighty eels. In the centre of the town a bridge spans the Corrib, and a couple of hundred yards upstream is a weir. When we arrived the water was too low for anything to get up the weir, and as we looked over the bridge, it seemed that the bottom was carpeted with salmon, sea-trout and some heroic eels. The whole place looked like a poacher's paradise, though it was presumably heavily supervised.

A fisherman was spinning down the stretch from the weir to the bridge and although we watched for half an hour, he did not connect. Indeed the fish were so dour that they barely moved. We were told in the pub afterwards that if anyone rented this expensive beat and by the end of the day looked like scoring a blank, the keeper would ask him to turn his back (a nice touch) and change the lure for something very heavy and with plenty of hooks. Having driven this equipage into a fish, he would hand the rod back to the client to play it.

Thirty odd years later on eels were responsible for one of the most frustrating incidents in my entire fishing experience. By this time I was married with four children, at this time ranging from about six to eleven. We were staying in a cottage on an idyllic estate on the west coast of Scotland. The cottage had originally been built for a gardener, apparently on the principle either that the view was too good for a servant or that he ought to be too busy to have time to look at it. Not a single window looked out over the rocks and beach to the sea loch, where seals bobbed about and an occasional sea-trout jumped.

At the top end of the loch a small burn fell in, and it was in the sea-pool, after some failed attempts in earlier years, that I finally managed to land three sea-trout, or to be precise, finnock. The biggest weighed less than a pound, but they were beautiful. I crept back into the cottage late that night and set them out on a plate for admiration by all in the morning. By that time a little starveling black cat which hung about the cottage had made an entry and eaten the head off the best fish.

It was decided (since all methods were allowed) that I would take the whole party up to the pool the following evening, armed with worms, spinners or whatever, while I tried again with the fly.

The expedition was an exercise in self-denial which I hope has been duly noted where it matters. Matthew had elected to spin with a little silver Mepps, but Sophie, James and Edward were worming. My rod was still in its case when the first little slimy horror came in. Then I had to go down and watch a flounder ponderously pursuing, but not taking, Matthew's spoon. Then back to deal with another eel, and so on. To cap it all, a breeze then got up and started to blow daddy-long-legs on the water; the sea trout took them keenly, with exciting boils and waves as they pursued the dipping and skating prey. This was too much; the children were abandoned to get on with things alone, and I scrabbled the tackle together. As the final knot was tied, the wind died away, and that was that.

One sure thing can be said for the eel; it is first-class eating. The same applied to the Broadlands salmon, and Father cynically observed that you never realised you had so many friends until word got round that you'd caught a good salmon. When he returned with one it was always laid out ceremonially on the dining-room table. People used to come in and admire it. Then it would be ceremoniously carved into chunks for presentation to those to be favoured on this occasion, the middle cut being the most honorific

The Broadlands water was always Father's main target, and here he spent what rather little time and money could be afforded for salmon fishing. He did, however, have one very substantial second string, which was the water in the War Memorial Park at Romsey. From his diary it appears that he rented this from about 1931 to 1939, and I remember his saying that the rent was £5 per annum. Even allowing for inflation, it must count as a sensational bargain.

Above the town of Romsey the Test breaks up into several streams. The main part goes down through Saddler's Mill, near which Walter Geary had his cottage. This was a good place for watching the salmon jump as they made their way upstream to annoy the riparian owners of the upper reaches. The remaining two branches came down on either side of the park, one very small, the other perhaps ten to fifteen yards across in the shallower places and even less where there was an occasional deep hole. All three constituents joined eventually about two hundred yards above the bridge which carried the road away from Romsey towards Southampton. Because of an island near the junction of the two minor streams they did not effectively join the main river until a point about thirty or forty yards from the final spit of land marking the end of Father's fishing. At least, it marked it, territorially speaking. It was possible to fish down below it, and nobody seemed to object to our doing so. On one bank some house and cottage gardens came down to the water, and on the other there was a public footpath from

Saddler's Mill to the road bridge, and this was never fished. Piscatorially it seemed to be a sort of no-go area for all except the fortunate tenant of the War Memorial Park fishing.

Father sometimes made trips especially to fish the Park, and sometimes used it as a back-up to a day at Broadlands. The water contained some tremendous trout and hefty grayling, with the ever-present chance of a salmon on the bigger of the two streams; they never seemed to run the little one. It was a curious place to fish and certainly would not have suited anyone whose idea of a crowded water is one with somebody fishing every quarter-mile. There were always people about in the Park and an incautious back-cast would bring angry cries from the passers-by or participants in the clock-golf. The hooking of any fish produced an immediate audience, and the longer it took to land, the bigger the attendance became. I've always been amazed by the capacity of almost any landscape to produce a crowd of onlookers when anything interesting starts to happen. Shortly after the war I was stationed in Palestine and went off to the Lebanon for my first and only attempt at ski-ing. This took place in the mountains right by the famous cedars, in what had been a training establishment until some genius by a stroke of the pen turned it into a leave camp. At the best of times it was far from comfortable, and when snow entirely blocked the single road up so that no supplies could reach us, became even less so. We arranged a supply drop by aircraft. As the containers fell into what had apparently been an entirely deserted landscape, human figures materialised from nowhere. Fortunately they were less interested in the containers than in the parachutes, of which we only recovered about half.

For salmon there were three main holding pools in the Park,

though it was not unknown for a fish to be picked up in other places. One deep hole was at the bottom, not far from the point, and it was here that the most famous Park salmon was taken.

It was in the summer of 1936 or 1937, and the liner Queen Mary was lying in Southampton harbour, open to the public like a floating stately home. My grandparents, Ralph and Alice Janes decided to make an outing, and took along me and Marcel Winter-Taylor. It was a boiling hot day. I certainly enjoyed the tour well enough but was all the time looking forward to the return journey, when the plan was that we would call in at the Park, where Father was fishing, to see how he was getting on.

Like the men at Galilee, he had toiled all day and caught nothing by the time our little party arrived at about four o'clock in the afternoon. My grandmother was no fishing expert; having come all this way she felt like seeing a little action.

"Do catch a salmon, Walter," she begged.

Father sighed, but once more unshipped his prawn and sent it off to explore, for the umpteenth time, the depths of the hole by the point. Against all the odds, and to his clear amazement, there came a heavy bump and he was into a lively fish. This was always a nerve-racking place to play a salmon because of the danger that it would set off downstream. This must have meant disaster, but in fact I don't think it ever happened.

Father, white as a sheet as usual, played the fish with deep concentration. After about five minutes, Granny began to get bored.

"Why don't you pull it out, Walter?"

Apart from a slight reddening of the neck, the first sign of any returning colour, Father managed not to react to this. Shortly afterwards, by which time I had darted up and fetched the park-

127

keeper to deal with the gaffing, a really nice bright fish of 11 lbs. came ashore to audience applause, the excited shrieks of small boys and the barking of dogs. As Father said afterwards, if the story had been written as fiction nobody would have believed a word of it.

Not far above this little pool there was another pot-hole which occasionally held a fish, and above that, on a sharp bend, was the Lavatory Pool. This was so called because the Ladies Lavatory stood on the bank here and it always seemed to me to be a toss-up whether one would connect with a fish before being arrested as a Peeping Tom. No doubt I needn't have worried. All the world knows that a fisherman, at least while fishing, has no room in his mind for anything else but the chase.

This attitude was well exemplified by a character in C. S. Forester's novel 'Flying Colours'. Captain Hornblower, captured in the Mediterranean after heroic exploits, is being escorted across France to Paris, for probable execution by the tyrant Bonaparte. Escaping, he fortunately finds himself in the house of M. le Comte de Gracay, no supporter of Napoleon, who helps him on his way. The plan is to travel down the Loire by boat. M. le Comte recommends that by way of disguise they take along fishing rods, saying:

"For some reason which I cannot analyse, a fresh water fisherman can never be suspected of evil intent – except possibly by the fish." Quite right too.

That more or less summed up the salmon lies, though a novice guest of Father's who knew no better was once fishing an apparently straight run above the Lavatory Pool and found himself playing a good fish. Although the bed of the river seemed featureless the bank, unfortunately, was not, and Mac Abbott spent a stimulating few minutes passing the rod back and forth to himself around the trunk of quite a stout tree. I know that he eventually lost it by a subsequent entry in my own first fishing diary, now lost, which records:

> "*Today I saw a man catch his first salmon at Broadlands. The man's name was Mr Mac Abbott.*"

Dull words for a momentous event. This was at the bottom end of No. 2 Beat.

Many of the big trout which were caught on the Park water came from the point of land at the very bottom end. They were not taken on the dry fly, and those who consider the Test sacred to this method should pass rapidly over the next page or two. They were not caught on wet fly either, not even the deadly Alexandra. Bread was what they took, and large lumps of it.

Where the three arms of the river rejoined about thirty or forty yards below the point in the Park, a lot of good fish lived a life undisturbed by any fishermen except us, and then only a few times a year. They had little time for duns, spinners and the like, and we never once saw a rise down there. There was no reason why these fish should rise, when the current brought down to them a stream of domestic delicacies from the town above, quite apart from the rich natural bottom feeding provided by the river itself.

Father's mechanical incompetence was undoubted, but he did have a certain flair for matching the gear to the occasion. When he had tired of trying to extract a salmon on the prawn, he simply removed the prawn and the lead, and put a large lump of bread on to the prawn hook. Maddeningly, I cannot now recall exactly how this was done, whether he used crust or pinched on a substantial piece of flake; certainly he never put himself to the trouble of making up paste. Crust seems the likeliest bet.

The bait was dropped into the current and allowed to trundle down to the confluence on a loose line. Every now and again a trout would take, and we were then, of course, equipped with just the sort of tackle which could handle a heavy trout hooked well downstream in a strong current. Even with the high-powered split cane rod then thought suitable for salmon, and with the rest of the tackle to match, it was extremely hard work.

I was once on the point with Father and his guest, Percy Goodearl, who had driven us down. Percy fished first and caught a lovely trout of 4¾ lbs. Then Father had a go and took one of close on 4 lbs. Finally, convinced that by now it must be all over, they allowed me to have a try, and eventually, puce with excitement and exertion, I landed one of 2¾ lbs. That in fact was my very first trout and should no doubt have spoiled me for the very large number of smaller fish which I caught before I ever got a bigger one. It didn't; a day or two later I was happily winkling out perch at Cookham.

All this may well be regarded by some as mere fishmongering. I do not recall Father expressing any moral doubts on the subject. His feeling, which seems eminently sound, was that in fishing, only three kinds of action are unsporting; anything which spoils the enjoyment of other people fishing the water; anything which causes unnecessary suffering to the fish; anything which damages the fishery itself. The rules of any water ought to be to try and ensure that all these are avoided. It may be that further regulation is also required, and a classic case is the 'dry-fly only' rule on some waters. If people come together who decide that the dry-fly method is what they prefer, and that that is how the (never unlimited) fish on their water will be caught, that is a perfectly reasonable decision, especially as it ensures that on the whole the fishers will be following one another upstream in an orderly way rather than having the wet and dry-fly exponents blundering into each other as they move in opposite directions. This decision is, however, practical and not moral; it certainly cannot make any difference to the fish how it is caught, except when a method is used which can cause it to be gut-hooked. This certainly did not apply to the bread-eaters of Romsey.

Not a million miles away from the Park water, at a very grand establishment, it was not unknown apparently for a method to be used which was at least as unorthodox as our own. Should a visiting notability arrive who had an interest in fishing but no great expertise (or perhaps even if he had expertise, but also a wholly understandable desire to catch a very large trout indeed) he would be escorted to a particular pool near the house and put to work, suitably equipped. It would subsequently be reported in the angling and local press that General This or the Bishop of That had taken a trout of some staggering weight on what was described as 'a local lure'. Our information was that this was a large lump of liver. The biggest caught there was, I believe, of the order of 18 lbs.

And why not, indeed? The people at this establishment, like Father in the Park, made the rules to suit themselves and the water. They did not offend against the principles of sportsmanship, and it's quite certain in the case of the bread enthusiasts that it would have been a minor miracle if any one of them ever succumbed to a fly, in the unlikely event of anyone solving the problem of putting one over them.

However, once away from the rather special circumstances of the point, the majority of the trout caught in the Park were in fact taken on the fly, and above all, the mayfly, with which great marvels

131

were always a reasonable hope.

Newly resurrected from my attic and mounted in a place of honour is a trout of 6 lbs. 14 oz., the largest of Father's career. This he caught in mayfly on May 21st 1933. Although it has been staring glassily from its case for more than fifty years now, it is in extremely good order.

This trout came from towards the tail of the Lavatory Pool where on the far bank, willows slightly overhung a lovely stretch of golden gravel. It may be imagination or advancing senility, but it does seem to me on the rare occasions when I now see the Test that it is not as clear now as it was then. Certainly in those days, a good fish sitting out on such gravel would be visible a long way off; when Father spotted this one it's easy to imagine the shortening of breath and the knocking of knees.

Although the fish itself is in good shape, the fly which the taxidermist put in its jaw has long since disintegrated. It's most likely that it was the favourite Barratt's Tar-Brush, though not, as will be seen, the one which actually took the fish.

The trout took almost immediately, and was eventually landed well down at the tail of the pool. Father, no doubt with trembling hands, despatched the fish. He was then staggered to find that an even larger trout had now appeared on the gravel run, and was already taking mayflies. He sprang into action, wrenched out the fly, gave it a quick rinse in the river and a few false casts to dry it, and covered the second monster. First cast, it stuck out an enormous nose and inhaled the fly. Alas, when Father tightened up, he felt the fish firmly for a brief moment, and then, as he always put it, 'it came unstuck'.

When he examined the fly, the point had gone. It may, of course, have broken off in the second fish, but there remained the strong and awful possibility, likelihood even, that he had broken the hook off in his haste to extract it from the first fish. Imagine offering a fly with no point to a fish which he estimated at possibly 9 lbs. Ever since then I have been a compulsive hook-sharpener and fly-examiner, and still manage to make a hash of it from time to time. Just recently I was fishing a slow pool with a shrimp imitation of some sort and had four sharp, fruitless takes before it occurred to me to take a proper look at the fly. A loop of the leader had snared the bend of the hook so that the fly was fishing backwards. This strange presentation had apparently not put the trout off at all; the next time I fished there, with everything set up as it should be, nothing was prepared to show any interest in the fly at all.

The strange thing about the 6 lbs. 14 oz. fish is its colouring, which is unlike that of any other trout I've ever seen. Overall the impression is of a rather dark fish. It has no red or pale spots, all are black, rather large and blotchy. The belly is distinctly pink, and there are black spots on the dorsal fin. None of this is due to any discolouration over the years; it has always been like that. The thought finally dawns that perhaps it is a rainbow, and that the colouring was the best try of a taxidermist who in that era may not have seen so very many of these. One day perhaps some expert will solve this problem. If indeed it is a rainbow, it would have been an excellent one for those days. My ancient copy of *Where to Fish* has gone astray but I'm sure that in the Notable Fish section the British record for a rainbow in the late thirties was some 8 lbs.

While Father was conducting the main operations in the Park, he left me to amuse myself by whatever method appealed, and this was all valuable experience. Float-fished worm brought trout up to

1½ lbs., and if I'd had the wit to use the method, a worm bumped along the bottom would surely have picked up a much better fish sooner or later. But in those days, for small boys and indeed for many of their seniors, bait-fishing meant float-fishing. Some beautiful grayling were also to be had. Another enjoyable ploy was to ply a one-inch gold or silver Devon minnow about the smaller of the two streams; Father never allowed this in our main stream because of the slim chance that a salmon might take hold; (presumably the risk with the worm was considered to be low because of the method of fishing it). I never had a trout of more than a pound on the mini-Devon minnow but it was exciting because the trout could sometimes be seen charging out from cover to take. No special spinning tackle was employed for all this, the minnow simply being tied on in place of the fly; casting, which only entailed a matter of three or four yards, was achieved by pulling off loose line and hoping it would not get entangled in the weeds.

All in all it was quite valuable experience, and not just in strictly piscatorial matters. Included were such character-forming experiences as playing a fish before an audience and losing it at the net, or of receiving for the eight time in the day the question 'Had any luck?' or the information that 'I haven't the patience for fishing.'

Strangely it was extremely near the Park water that I caught my first, and indeed only, salmon. An advertisement appeared in the classified section of Angling Times to the effect that a day-ticket could be obtained for trout and salmon-fishing on the Test at Romsey at a charge, in those pre-decimal days of 1962, of thirty shillings, or £1.50. It was clear that at this price it couldn't possibly be any good, equally clear that however poor it might be I was bound to have a try. The agents were contacted and a day fixed for about the middle of May. The map which accompanied the ticket showed that the water was immediately above the War Memorial Park, and indeed car-parking turned out to be in a side road in sight of the upper bridge.

The weather was hot so I set off early and was standing by the river, ready to start, at eight in the morning. One reason for the low cost of the ticket was immediately apparent; the water was divided into an upper and a lower beat, and neither was much more than a hundred yards long.

Motivated by a sense of history I had armed myself with some prawns. Father scorned any but English prawns but by this time it appeared that fishmongers could not guarantee the provenance of their wares and my little bag-full might have come from anywhere. Not many possessed the heavy load of eggs which was also apparently a desirable feature, though it seemed doubtful that they can have survived more than a few casts however carefully the prawn was mounted.

Despite the passage of some twenty years since it was last demonstrated I remembered the prawn-mounting drill quite well, possibly because with the exception of shoe-cleaning (of his own shoes, anyway) it was about the only time Father did anything requiring any manual dexterity, apart from the actual casting, shooting or wicket-keeping. First the prawn was very gently unbent from its curled state. Then the baiting needle went in underneath the tail and was very carefully pushed through to come out at the lead. The nylon (in my case) was pulled through and tied to the hook, which was then drawn up to nestle snugly among the prawn's whiskers. A cocktail stick was then inserted by way of a splint to keep the prawn's body straight, and the treatment completed by winding the whole thing with copper wire to make all fast, taking great pains to leave all the little legs dangling. All this went according to plan, with the daring innovation of a treble hook instead of the large single which Father used to use, the logic of which I never had been able to follow. Nobody dreamed of using a single hook on a Devon minnow. The spool of copper wire was the same as had been used at Broadlands in pre-war days. Unlike a lot of our gear it survived all war-time moves and upheavals, and is still in use today for Pheasant-Tail nymphs.

As all this was completed, there was a sudden heavy swirl in the river immediately opposite where I was standing. The whole outing on this mini-beat seemed so preposterous that even then it didn't seem likely that this could truly be a salmon – a pike perhaps; they were certainly about in the water. All the same, I lobbed the prawn out and as it swung over the spot there was a heavy thump, and away we went. Even then I couldn't believe it was a salmon – but it was. After some alarming moments when it took off downstream where I couldn't follow I managed to scramble it out, after one bungled gaffing attempt which I'm ashamed of to this day. It was a most beautiful fish, 11 lbs. as it turned out, one of the small fish of the summer run which it appears from Father's diary started to overlap the big spring fish some time in April.

His average fish for February and March weighed 22½ lbs. not that there were all that many of them. Add in the April results, a mixture of small summer and big spring fish and the average drops to not quite 19 lbs. From May onwards the figure is a little over 14 lbs. In May 1932 he had fish of 9 lbs. and 13 lbs. from what he notes as the Piscatorial Society water, which was very near to, and may well have included, the little stretch where my one and only triumph took place.

So, by 8.15 a.m. on this May day, thirty years after Father had scored perhaps from that very spot, I had a salmon tucked away under the rushes to keep cool, and was eating a prawn by way of celebration.

At this point a splendid, if indignant, figure appeared from downstream, exquisitely turned out in tweed and waterproofs.

"Excuse me," he shrilled, "but you are fishing in water on which I have exclusive rights."

This is never a particularly agreeable situation, but having spent a careful few minutes around the boundary of the two tiny beats I felt reasonably confident, and managed to convince the new arrival after a few minutes that in fact it was he who was invading the area on which I had 'exclusive rights'. We fell into pleasant talk and eventually (and fortunately, otherwise it would have been necessary to force the conversation that way) he asked me whether there had been any action. A movement of the boot revealed the still-shining silver flank of the noble creature; it was a very good moment indeed. Strangely it turned out that my neighbour had not brought any salmon-tackle along, and he kindly invited me to use mine on his beat, a generous way of making up for his earlier pounce.

Later in the day an old man appeared who turned out to be the part-time bailiff of the stretch. He told me that they reckoned to get about eight fish a year, and pointed out a couple of holding places which one would have been extremely lucky to find without such help. The prawn came back from a visit to one of these looking distinctly mangled, but without my feeling anything at my end. This could well have been another salmon just giving the bait an exploratory pinch.

At the time the old man came along to talk, I had temporarily changed over to trout-tackle to have a go at a fish that was rising fairly well out in the stream. He was just recounting how the trout-fishing was really of negligible account on this particular stretch when the fish tipped up and took the Lunn's Particular down with great confidence. It turned out to weigh 1¾ lbs., and completed a day not only of success but of dramatically-witnessed success, something that I openly admit to enjoying on the rather rare occasions that it comes about – goodness knows, there are plenty of the other sort.

The fishing in the Park at Romsey was always rather special for me. After all, there cannot be many places where you can catch a salmon, buy a bag of crisps and watch a game of tennis, all within a few yards, as you could in those days.

Some of the diary entries about the Park water may give the feel of it.

May 4th 1931

> *"Before breakfast, with the aid of the baker, caught a fine trout of 3 lbs. 12 oz. in the Park."*

May 21st 1933

> *"To Romsey with Drs. Craig and Gillespie. Mayfly hatching, but not very well. Caught about 20 and killed 6, one a fine fish that weighed 6 lbs. 14oz. hours after capture – he was undoubtedly over 7 lbs. Dr. Gillespie let him fall out of the net once, and when he did net it, the net collapsed."*

May 18th 1935

> *"To Romsey with Mac Abbott. 10.55 train from Wycombe. 12.30*

from Waterloo – lunch on the train. Left Southampton West at 1.59 – Romsey 2.30. Down to the Park – hooked a 12 lb. salmon at the bottom, first cast. On Sunday, got a 5 lbs. 2 oz. trout on prawn".

May 25th 1935

"Missed a salmon in Lavatory Pool. Got a fine 4 lbs. 15 oz. trout on Mayfly".

May 9th 1937

"On Sunday, got a 17 lbs. salmon in the Park. Netted by four small boys who appeared, luckily, when I thought the Park was empty."

May 21st 1938

"Killed a decent fish of 4 lbs. 12 oz. on Mayfly in the Park. He was in full view at the bottom and was nymphing, but was bullied into rising. He got down into the main stream, when I found a knot in the line. The reel came off, and the park-keeper missed him twice with the net, but we got him in the end."

Chapter Ten

West Wycombe Park lies to the west of High Wycombe from which the approach is made by a dramatically straight road, without a bend for two miles. This road was made by the first Sir Francis Dashwood, using the chalk excavated from the caves which he caused to be bored deep into the hillside. Whether the digging out of the caves or the construction of the road was the main objective is disputed.

On top of the hill stands the Church of St. Lawrence, surmounted by its golden globe, which was added to the original structure by Sir Francis, and the Mausoleum, which he also built. The whole effect is highly dramatic, whether seen by daylight with the sun reflected on the globe, or by night, when the Mausoleum is floodlit. The reverse view, the town seen from the Mausoleum, is also sensational.

Sir Francis, was, of course, the prime mover of the infamous Hell Fire Club, whose gambling, wenching, drinking, blasphemy and general debauchery, though fascinating, are of no concern here. One might observe that anyone who could achieve much in the way of sinning inside the golden ball on top of West Wycombe church probably deserved all the thrills he could get. It is now too dangerous for public access, but as a small boy I went up into it. Apart from its cramped discomfort it was a fairly frightening place, with distinct overtones of 'Nearer, my God, to thee.'

West Wycombe House dates back to before 1700, but like most

similar houses has been re-modelled from time to time. It is a fine building of pale yellow stone, with an unusual double-deck colonnade on the south side. Fishermen, however, get a view only of the north side which overlooks the most attractive lake formed by Humphrey Repton by damming two little streams. This occurred after the death of Sir Francis in 1781, and a great deal of other landscaping was done at the same time.

The result is a most attractive scene. The lake covers about nine acres, including an island near the shore in front of the house, and reached by a little flint and stone bridge. This accommodates the boat house. In the middle of the lake is another island on which stands the 'Music Room', a temple-like colonnaded structure with a domed roof. Each feeder stream enters the lake through an ornamental bridge, again of flint and stone. It is hardly possible now to see that the lake was originally made by damming, but slightly off-centre of that dam the water leaves the lake by an ornamental waterfall, flanked by statuary of reclining female figures, presumably nymphs. The water flows over a sloping apron, with dragons' teeth to break the flow decoratively.

From there a stream takes the water first down a straight stretch, then in two long curves, with miniature weirs in places. Finally it comes up against another long dam to make a long pool, and two sluices divide it back to two streams again. By one sluice stands the Sawmill House, an attractive brick and flint building, and here the water has been widened to make a final, round, pool.

According to one theory the lake, the curving stream, and the final pool, when seen from the top of West Wycombe Hill, form an image of the swan which is High Wycombe's emblem. With the eye of faith, it's possible to catch the resemblance.

The water at West Wycombe is of the most extreme clarity; the fishermen can see a trout a very long way off indeed, and the reverse, of course, is also the case. But the water has a long history of going dry from time to time, and it would appear that it did so in 1935, or possibly earlier. By 1936 it had refilled, and was stocked with yearling trout of about six to eight inches. The following year the water was left unfished, and by the 1938 season, it contained some big fish, at least by the standards of those days when it was unheard-of to rear trout to enormous weights before putting them in.

The fishing was leased at that time to Father's cousins, Frank and Ted Gomme, who were now the reigning proprietors of the furniture business in High Wycombe with which my paternal grandfather had earlier been associated, and for which Father now worked. It seems quite on the cards that it was he who put Ted and Frank up to the idea that it would be a good ploy to take on the fishing, and certainly he was at least as keen on it as they were.

Whatever the origins of the lease, it was an extremely worthwhile one. Apart from the peace, beauty and historical associations of the place, the quality of the trout-fishing was tremendous. In 1939 Father fished at West Wycombe eleven times and these would almost always have been short evening jaunts rather than all-day affairs. He took sixteen trout, which averaged 2¾ lbs. The best fish, caught on September 17th, weighed 4 lbs. 10½ oz. and he had another one of over 4 lbs. on June 30th. On June 3rd, using what he describes as a 'cut-down Mayfly' he had a bag of four fish, the best 3¼ lbs. and averaging over 2½ lbs. During the whole season he only killed four trout of less than 2 lbs., but returned many more. From my own memory, all these fish were in first-rate condition, as indeed they must have been to have got to such weights in the time.

The old treatises on the management of fish ponds set great store on the virtues of a dry period, to the point where in some cases the fisheries could be totally drained and returned to arable cropping for a while. The dry period certainly did this water no harm at all in the long run, and the quantities of excellent body-building food such as shrimp and snail were impressive. So far as I know the regeneration of these after the drought was quite natural and there was no need for them to be re-introduced. They produce a trout whose splendid red flesh owed nothing to the introduction of crushed shrimp or whatever it is that goes into the trout-pellets these days.

On the debit side, there was not and is not now a good population of ephemerids. An occasional olive or sedge may be observed, but there is no mayfly, B.W.O., or any of the other flies on which the classic chalk-streams depend for sport with the dry fly, or at least not in such numbers as to make them worth taking into a fisherman's calculations. This does not mean that the trout do not rise; they do and violently at times, but the puzzle is to discover on what. Any fish taken during such a rise is likely to be full of tiny snails, and it may well be that this is all they are taking, as the snails drift down, foot-up, in the surface film. Chironomids, and the Hawthorn fly in its season, can also get the trout going, as can the flies which hatch from rafts of floating algae. But the basic diet of the West Wycombe fish has always been shrimp, snail and other such sub-aqueous fare.

My first forays to this water were, of course, made in the capacity of bag-carrier, errand boy and general hanger-on. It was far more entertaining than doing the same job elsewhere, mainly because the water was so astoundingly clear. Fish-watching is a pastime that for me will never pall, and here it was at its best. It was almost like being in the water alongside them. At the top end of the fishery, the elegant little bridge spanning the main feeder streams has a low parapet , not more than eighteen inches high. Wandering off one day I crept up to the middle of this and very cautiously stuck my head over. Immediately below was the most beautiful trout I'd ever seen, yellow as a guinea, every spot visible, and apparently enormous. The current was not fast, and he was gently cruising to collect his dinner, a shrimp here and a snail there. His white mouth could clearly be seen as it opened to take something in, this often followed by a couple of jaw movements as he crushed whatever it was. From time to time he broke surface, probably to take something from the tree which overhung there. It did not dawn on me until later that it was only the dark background provided by this tree which had prevented the fish from bolting immediately my head appeared over the parapet.

It was a lesson well learned. Much later in life I gained access to one short but excellent pool on the Wylye, in Wiltshire. It was immediately below the bridge at Longbridge Deverill, and the old lady who had the cottage there used to let me fish for 1/6d. an evening, about 7½p. The whole extent of the fishing was less than twenty yards, but it was an ideal place to go after a day's work on the farm, or even after an evening's cricket after a day's work on the farm. One of the great advantages was that there was a hedge close up to the water at the top end. As soon as it ceased to be full daylight it was possible to stand against this hedge and vanish altogether from the sight of the trout which lay in the plum positions under and just below the bridge. My diary is only complete for 1955; here it records thirteen visits for twenty-one fish, of which fifteen were kept and six returned. The fifteen killed averaged 1 lb. 2 oz. Almost every fish fell for the Lunn's Particular, which must be one of the most effective all-round dry flies ever tied. A substantial number of all these trout were caught while taking advantage of the background cover of the hedge. The total should, needless to say, have been much higher. This was at the height (or more realistically, depth) of a really bad period of 'striker's twitch'; on May 22nd 1955, the first attempt of the season, the diary records bleakly "Missed fourteen, one after the other."

West Wycombe in the thirties boasted only one boat, and a perfect little swine it was. Curiously constructed of corrugated iron over a wooden frame, it was shaped like a short, fat punt, square at both ends. It drew practically no water at all and the lightest puff of wind would set it scuttling off across the surface like a water-skater. The dropping of so much as a pair of scissors produced a reverberating clang audible by a trout half-way across the lake. A more unsuitable craft for this water could hardly have been conceived. The super-clear water made it theoretically possible to spot an individual fish thirty yards or more away, and to stalk it. The practice was quite another thing.

Father was out on the lake one day being ghillied for by my mother, not an expert boatman at the best of times, which this was not. As the little breezes suddenly blew, so the boat would bear down on some enormous trout that a few moments before had been cruising peacefully along the edges of the weed-beds. Father's temper always operated on a dangerously short fuse and, after about the fifth trout had been put down there came the inevitable explosion. With a screech of rage he hurled the rod into the water. This, needless to say, rolled off Mother's knife altogether – she wasn't doing the fishing and was quite prepared to sit there indefinitely enjoying the view (and, quite possibly Father's rage). Impasse. For once Father was tree'd, and after they had twirled sedately round this way and that for a few minutes he had to give in, apologize, and get the operation under way once more. The rod was in less than three feet of water and reasonably easily retrieved, and indeed I wonder whether this dramatic demonstration would have occurred had they been over deep water at the time.

I also suffered from this hellish craft, or rather my 'client' did so. This was Colonel Peter Hammond, a colleague of Father's from the Piscatorial Society, a ballistics expert and extremely fine fisherman. He was tall, thin, and at first appearance, morose. In fact, he could be extremely diverting, with a sardonic turn of humour; he just wasn't a chatterbox. To a small boy he was something of an awesome figure, to start with at least, and it was with a good deal of trepidation that I found myself detailed to take the great man out in the boat on the lake.

It was the very worst sort of day for the job. There was a good light, making fish-spotting easy, but at the same time gusty winds kept springing up with the worst possible effect on the horrible punt. The whole performance was a disastrous repeat of the Father/Mother episode except in the reaction of the fisherman. An explosion of rage was just not P.H.'s style, but even I could see, as we drove over the top of about the third good fish and it bolted into the weed, that he didn't care for it. He slowly and carefully laid the rod down across the punt and quietly, but with deadly emphasis, said " — the — wind!" He then lit his pipe and started off again. Not another word was said, but it was not very long before we were back on the bank.

On another occasion in that year P.H. put up the finest

performance of the season by catching three trout in an evening, all over four pounds. But before this took place, I briefly held the stage, and the record, with a fish of 4¼ lbs. This was in 1938, and is immortalised by an entry in *The Sketch* of July 13th that year; a photocopy is before me, the cutting itself having long since disintegrated.

The journal, a weekly, ran a page called *When I was last a-fishing*, written by a well-known angling author of the time, R.L. Marston. Much of the material came in from correspondence, not only in this country. In the same issue Mr G.F. Wooliams wrote to tell of the fishing at Denton Bridge, Bathurst, Gambia, "a favourite spot for anglers both European and native. The bridge is a narrow one and dangerous owing to motor traffic." Apparently the reaction of the authorities to this state of affairs was not to prohibit angling but to post up a notice: "No vehicle is to pass over this bridge while angling is going on. Non-observance of this prohibition will be met by rigid prosecution."

From the centre of the page glowers a small figure in heavily crumpled grey school suit holding out what even in a poor photograph, and after photocopying, was a really lovely fish.

R.L. Marston reports:

> *"In the throes of the Test Match Mr Pierce writes to tell me that his son Roger, aged thirteen, killed a trout of 4¼ lbs. in some private water on June 10th. Roger, I might add, is no novice, having many large trout to his credit, and he landed this one in half an hour."*

The bit about "having many large trout to his credit" is a piece of pure Father-style hyperbole, but the half-hour taken to land the fish is unbelievably, something near the truth. Never before or since have I been connected to a fish for so long.

Guest-tickets for the water were highly prized, quite rightly, and had an appearance to match. They were printed on heavy white card, with the recipient's name handsomely hand-written by the chief secretary at the furniture factory. When one finally arrived for me, personally, it occupied a place of honour in my bedroom just like any grand invitation casually sported on the chimneypiece by the grown-ups.

This time, instead of my doing the rowing and bag-carrying, Father was to be in this role while I did the fishing, using his best split-cane rod, what's more. When we got to the lake and set off, the wind for once was not troublesome, and although there was nothing much going on in the way of a general rise, it was easy to see fish moving. The main weed was marestail and following the drying-up, this was coming back in clumps and patches with plenty of clear water in between. The fish spent most of their time foraging about the weed patches, and as they moved from one to another they were very clearly visible against the pale silt of the bottom.

The stand-by fly popular at that time was the Invicta, which to this day still does the trick quite regularly and will no doubt continue to do so. Commonly reckoned to be a sedge pupa imitation it seems unlikely to be taken for this at West Wycombe where sedges are only occasionally seen. For whatever reason the trout appreciate it, and this is what we put up. There was no great subtlety about the fishing of it; you simply cast, and fetched it back in a succession of tweaks and pulls. If it fell close to a fish it would probably be taken as it sank, without any movement.

We set off, and almost immediately I was into a good fish which came unstuck. Clearly this was to be a day of action, but unfortunately not quite as one would have wished. For an hour and a half, I flogged away, getting more and more agitated, casting going all to pieces, as a succession of disasters overtook me. Fish were missed, or were hooked and lost in the weeds; huge targets would appear and drift slowly past while I struggled to get myself out of a tangle, only to vanish as all came straight. Overhanging branches sprang sideways to intercept the fly. It was quite apparent that no matter whose name was on the ticket, it was only a matter of time before Father lost patience and took over.

At this point we were just by the boat-house island. Close to the shore was a horse-shoe-shaped patch of weed, forming a little lagoon perhaps a couple of yards across. Framed in this was the best trout we had seen so far, poling gently across from one side to the other. As they say ". . . cometh the hour, cometh the man . . ." (or in this case, boy). Everything suddenly came good, and the fly dropped neatly, about a foot in front of the fish. Consonant with the dignity of such a monster, there was no sign of excitement, no vulgar acceleration. the trout simply continued on its stately way and at the appropriate moment, opened a large pink mouth to take the victim in. Crushing down the prevailing tendency at such moments to give a loud screech and snatch the fly neatly from its jaws, I waited until the mouth was well closed before tightening up.

The fish was off like a rocket, the cast slicing through some surface weed, and we were off into the deeper water. It was now apparent that, however undeservedly, some of the previous mis-managements were about to pay off. My previous tribulations had resulted in the loss of the entire gut point from my leader not once but several times. Father had got fed up with replacing them, so a fly was now tied to the main part of the leader probably about 2X, and not a bit too stout at that for the work now in hand. With a heavy fish, plenty of weed and an inexperienced hand on the rod, you need all the strength you can get.

Possibly it was not really half an hour. Certainly it seemed like an age, and at one point there is no doubt that the fish did actually move the punt; not so surprising perhaps, given the minimal draught of the craft, but impressive all the same. In the end, the fish tired and gave Father a simple job with the net. At 4¼ lbs. it was an absolute corker; even in the dim photograph its small head and great depth can be clearly seen.

I have no recollection at all of what happened after that. Perhaps the experience was so climactic that we just packed up and went home, or possibly Father took over the fishing, leaving me on the bank to gloat.

The trout was not quite of a size to qualify for an expensive glass case. Instead, Miss Groom at the factory, a talented artist, painted a picture of it for me. Sadly, that picture was one casualty of war-time moves and upheavals, and was never seen after about 1944.

The fish itself was eaten at a triumphant supper at Lansdowne School in High Wycombe where I was then a weekly boarder, and very good it was too. The weekly boarding was supposed to be a preparation for full boarding school the following term and I found it a highly satisfactory arrangement, allowing cricket during the week and fishing plus home comforts at the week-end.

The last possible ounce of excitement and enjoyment was squeezed from the episode by entering the trout for the Dry Fly sherry award, then offered by Williams and Humbert for a trout of over 4 lbs. The sherry duly appeared, accompanied by a pleasant letter saying that as Father would no doubt be taking charge of the sherry, (he did), they were enclosing an extra present, just for me. This turned out to be an ingenious pocket comb, inside a metal case, from which it emerged when a knob on the top was slid sideways. The disordered hair of the small figure in the photograph betrays no sign that the comb was ever likely to see much action, but it is, of course, the thought that counts.

One splendid figure who regularly visited West Wycombe was Colonel Freddy Cripps, brother of the better known Sir Stafford. The latter, whether or not with justification, was firmly established in the public minds as austere, ascetic and an all-round killjoy. His appointment as a minister in the war-time coalition government contributed to this, and his appearance with thin face, sharp nose and glasses enabled cartoonists everywhere to reinforce the impression. Colonel Cripps was a different cup of tea, and his own autobiography makes it quite clear that in temperament he more resembled the mythical King Cachoo in one of the ballads sung by Frank Crummit, who

> ". . . *loved to chase the bounding stag*
> *Within the royal wood;*
> *He was also fond of applejack,*
> *And the ladies did him good.*"

I was once able to render Colonel Cripps a small service by netting a good trout for him in the pool below the cascade. Father and I had been standing at a respectful distance watching him ply what even to my inexperienced eyes was a very curious confection indeed, a dry Alexandra apparently. It was unusual not merely in its style but in its enormous size, and as it floated down, brilliant in green and scarlet it resembled nothing so much as a dead kingfisher. This particular trout, however, found all this quite in order and sucked it in cheerfully. Of course, any big trout with a heavy body to sustain must look kindly on any opportunity to get a big mouthful with a small effort.

Almost exactly thirty years later on the opening day of the season I set off after a big fish, marked down in the river during the close season. He was lying in a narrow channel, behind what was then called Rat Island. My first shot landed in a bush, but he took the Black and Peacock Spider at the second attempt. His weight was exactly four pounds, and inside he contained one large frog.

One of the drawbacks on the river at West Wycombe arises from the fact that the whole thing is artificial. It was made not for fishing but to please the eighteenth century eye for landscaping. The trouble is that even when the flow of water is at its best, the stream is in many places too wide to produce any speed of current. The result is a series of long pools rather than a conventional chalk stream. None the less, wherever the water comes over the dams there is good gravel, and the trout take full advantage of this for spawning. They also boldly run the feeder streams from the lake, and the result is that given a reasonable period without the water going dry, there is a most satisfactory population of home-bred brown trout which have never seen the inside of a fish farm and don't know what a trout-pellet looks like.

It is, moreover, not only the brown trout which spawn. Creeping about the feeder streams it is possible from time to time to spot little rainbows of only a few inches long which have certainly never been stocked at that size. At one time it was quite usual occasionally to catch in the lake a half-pound rainbow which, apart from its small size, in no way resembled the stock fish, being bright silver with very little red and very few spots. It is unlikely that such fish themselves go on to breed and form a self-sustaining population, but the fact that they appear at all is pleasing.

According to Father's diary, he only fished once more at West Wycombe after the war started. This was on May 4th 1943. It seems to have been an action-packed outing, with five fish averaging just under 2 lbs., the best 3¼ lbs., all brown trout and all from the lake. Though it is recorded that I caught one of 2 lbs. and lost another, I have no recollection whatever of this expedition. Judging by the date it must have been laid on as a special treat immediately before I went off to the army. The diary shows that we were sharing one rod; this pleasant custom can be highly beneficial for the young, it would be nice to see it allowed on more fisheries, even if it were confined only to young members of the rod's family.

After my war-time visit, twenty-five years passed before I was able to visit West Wycombe again, by which time Father was long since dead.

The diary reference to West Wycombe are rather sparse, and in any case more urgent matter intervened with the outbreak of war in September. Here are a few entries:

May 28th 1938

> "*To West Wycombe with Roger. Rained like hell, but had good sport and killed four fish, 3 of 2 lbs. and one of 2 lbs. 12 ozs.*"

June 30th 1939

"Got one of the big trout at the top of the lake after much changing of flies. 4 lbs. 2 oz."

September 17th 1939

"After losing one and missing two, got a wonderfully conditioned fish of 4 lbs. 10½ oz. in the lake. Tom Thurlow says it is the best fish he has ever seen. Length 20", girth 14½" and very thick."

Chapter Eleven

Father had an enviable capacity for making friends, who seemed to come in all shapes and sizes. By no means all of these met with the approval of the family. One, indeed, was always referred to as 'that dreadful Alf', never with more feeling than after the occasion when the two of them were returning late from some foray in Alf's van, and a hare appeared on the road in front of them. In the daft way of hares it set off at a smart pace with Alf in full cry behind. When it eventually did have the sense to turn off the road, so did the van, and the whole equipage finished on one of the fairways of Temple Golf Club.

Alf (not, needless to say, his real name) also featured in the immersion of the Marlow postman. Father and he set off one warm summer night in a punt, armed with a wind-up gramophone and various records. As they paddled gently up towards Temple Lock, they played away, and no doubt occasionally took a little something to keep out the cold as the night fell deeper. The records which were unfavourably received were used for playing ducks-and-drakes. Somehow or other it was dawn when the party returned, moored the punt, and set off back over the suspension bridge.

It was here that they fell in with the postman. Accounts vary as to whether the deed was achieved by threats, physical force or bribery though it was almost certainly the latter. Whichever way the meeting ended with the postman going in off the bridge, fully clothed. It then appeared that his prowess at swimming was not all it might be; Father had to get in after him smartly and tow him to the bank before he joined the swans in the weir pool.

Other friends were less disreputable. At least one, indeed, was rich. This was the one whose expensive tackle I had put at risk by tangling with one of the swans at Marlow. John (let's say) was one of the kindest men imaginable, with, none the less, that healthy appreciation of the difference between *meum* and *tuum* that presumably is one of the qualities which makes one rich in the first place. His money had been earned in some form of manufacturing, and once the pile was made (and breeding away in the happy way that good investments do, so they tell me) he entered the realm of field sports. It was unkindly said that his only motivation was a form of social climbing, but I never thought that was so. He did genuinely seem to enjoy both fishing and shooting; the trouble was that he was completely hopeless at both.

He took a gun in the same syndicate as Father and soon was labelled by the beaters, 'Mr Bang-Bang', since no bird ever fell to his first shot; all too seldom to the second either, as a matter of fact. Peter Hammond was shooting as a guest one day; as the guns gathered at the end of one drive, one of them happened to say:

"Were you standing at this corner last time, John?"

Before John could reply Peter Hammond interjected in his staccato way:

"Couldn't have been him."

"Why not?"

"Odd number of cartridge cases."

John took it all in good part, as he did all the considerable amount of leg-pulling which came his way on sporting occasions.

Where fishing was concerned I came across John most often at

Broadlands. Generally he hired the beat and took Father along as guest, guide and mentor; if it happened to be in the school holidays I was allowed to go as well.

We travelled in the most terrific style, in the Rolls. This would be chauffeured by James (again, let's call him), a sardonic individual whose attitude to his employer was a mixture of genuine liking and respect, exasperation and near-insolence. In fact, he got away with murder, but at the same time really did his best to look after the guv'nor, whether as chauffeur, valet, ghillie or general factotum.

Discretion, however, was not among his virtues. He gleefully told me a splendid story one day about a partridge drive . . . It took place in the Chilterns, and the guns stood down the length of a long hill, so that No. 1 was about a hundred and fifty feet higher than John, at No. 8. On the flank, coming along the top of the hill was a walking gun, who shot at a bird which was breaking away to the flank. The bird swung forward but was well hit, and started to tower. It reached its apogee just as it arrived over John; by that time it was about three hundred feet up and, of course, stone dead. John's gun swung up and, for once, there was one shot. The bird continued its earthward plunge and John turned to James.

"That's the way to kill 'em, James."

Back to Broadlands. On arrival, the boot would be opened to reveal quantities of expensive gear. It is my only encounter with rods encased not in cloth bags but in fitted leather cases, like gun-cases. Possibly more important was the hamper, reminiscent of that of the Rat and Mole except for the substitution of whisky and wine for the ginger beer and lemonade. James took care of setting all this out in readiness for lunch, while the two rods went their ways on to the beat.

As usual, the hirer of the beat owned all fish caught, whether by him, his guest, or a keeper. On one occasion Father struck rather good form and when it was time to re-assemble for lunch, he had two good fish laid out on the grass by the fishing hut. John appeared a moment or two later and his eyes lit up.

"Well done, Walter. I'll tell you what – if you catch another one you can have it."

But this was only a first impulse. In the event, no more fish were caught, and Father still went home with one.

I was not there, of course, every time that John and Father fished together but, according to Father, John only once ever got a fish on the bank. Even then, tragi-comedy overtook him. By some extraordinary mischance, he was alone when he hooked the fish and his shouts raised neither James nor the keeper. By some heroic effort he managed to beach the fish and to scramble it up the bank. Here he unhooked it and stood back to gaze in admiration, most understandably, at his first, possibly only, salmon. Unfortunately he had failed to realize that a good hard blow on the fish's head with a blunt instrument is an essential preliminary to the safe savouring of such moments. As Father, who had in fact heard the shouts, came hurrying up to join in the celebrations, the fish gave a sudden leap, and slithered back down the bank into the river, to vanish immediately from sight.

Peter Hammond's encounters with John were fairly infrequent, though even so probably not infrequent enough for P.H. The most hideous of these took place once again at Broadlands. It was during the Mayfly and P.H. had located a truly enormous trout at the bottom of No. 2 Beat, just above the cattle bridge. He set about this fish with typical patience, thoroughness and determination, getting himself into a casting position, difficult but the best available, some time before the hatch was expected. He did not want to risk putting the fish down by crawling in among the willows after it had taken up its feeding position. As a soldier he knew the value of stillness and concealment. Certainly, when John, by a most unfortunate chance arrived on the other bank, he had no idea at all that P.H. was there. The latter did not reveal himself; never at any time loquacious, he hoped that John would pass on his way.

No such luck. At that moment, the monster moved out on to its gravel patch, probably in response to the movement of the first nymphs. That produced the first piece of bad luck. Normally John would not have spotted the fish in a month of Sundays, but this time he did. Then came the second misfortune. For John, accurate casts were generally as rare as snowflakes in May, but again, not this time. His very first cast, with a substantial plug bait, landed square on the trout's head. As the ripples died away, the gravel patch was empty. John went on his way up the bank, delighted with a good cast at what he almost certainly thought was a salmon, and still quite unaware of P.H.'s presence on the other bank. P.H. said not a word to him, then or later, but did sadly recount the incident to Father.

I refer to him as 'P.H.' simply because the 'Colonel Hammond' which was my invariable way of addressing him when I was a boy seems after all these years too formal for someone who in his own quiet and reserved way was always extremely kind and encouraging to me. (He and Father, of course, addressed each other as Hammond and Pierce for quite a few years before first names were allowed to creep in). On several occasions he took me fishing with him. The first time was at the Piscatorial Society water on the Gade in Hertfordshire, from which he extracted two excellent trout, using the most delicate and anonymous-looking dry flies. He was, however, by no means interested only in fly-fishing, and one day took three really splendid perch of around 1½ lbs. each from the Kennet, using a copper spoon. They made a tremendous impression on me, and I still think they are just about the handsomest of fish. Certainly a good perch looks every ounce of its weight, and it has been delightful after the years of the horrid perch disease to see their recovery, and some really hefty fish being reported in the fishing papers.

Much of my early tackle was the gift of P.H. The Allcock's Hexacane has already been referred to, but he also let me have a good 9-foot greenheart, as well as some ancient fly-wallets filled with glorious wet flies, all without eyes and tied directly on to gut links. Even then they were old-fashioned, but beautiful and interesting. No doubt they would now be collector's items, but all have long since vanished. An even sadder loss is the small stock of Hardy catalogues which made enthralling reading even then, and would do so even more now. I loved the illustrations, apparently woodcuts, which set out all the gear to which we hoped one day to aspire.

At the very end of the war I was stationed on Salisbury Plain, billeted in what I think had been the vicarage of the village of Figheldean. Round the grounds ran the excellent Avon. P.H., arranged for me to fish the river as his guest on what I think must even then have been the Officers' Fishing Association water, or its equivalent. Immediately behind the house was a pool which was completely overhung by the most enormous hawthorn, whose branches trailed almost into the water in a dense canopy. In its shadow, good trout would cruise about consuming the various dainties which from time to time missed their footing, beetles, woodlice and the like.

The rule of the fishing was, of course, dry-fly only. But it seemed to me that it was quite impossible to cast to these fish in the orthodox and accepted upstream way, because of the barrier of thorny twigs. The only way was to dibble a fly from above, while lying along the trunk of the tree. It's hard to believe that, be the fly never so dry, such a procedure would then have been considered dubious by quite a few of the true dry-fly men. There was, however, worse to come. War-time and youth are both inimical to moral standards and before long I had persuaded myself that in the circumstances there was very little difference between a hackled Alder and a grasshopper. There were plenty of these in the long grass, and stalking them with a rolled-up newspaper was quite a little field-sport in its own right. (Another lesser field-sport was developed by Matthew. He had a number of toads located in hidey-holes about the garden. They seemed to have no fear of him, and would sit quite placidly in his palm while he carried them round the windows, zapping the house flies with their long tongues. Rather like falconry, though, of course, slower.)

Dapping the grasshopper was extremely exciting work. The drill was to stand at the base of the tree, then lower the body on to the trunk. The grasshopper was then paid out to dangle an inch or two above the water in the part of the pool where the reflection afforded good visibility. Then it was a matter of waiting until suddenly there would be a trout in the target area. Quite often it would already have spotted the grasshopper and be eyeing it beadily. This was the moment to lower away, the nerves steeled to avoid snatching it away too soon. The approach of the trout varied from the nervous violent dash to the almost unbearably slow suck. Once fisherman and fish were connected there came the problem of extracting it from all the undergrowth.

Inevitably there came the dreadful day when I was stretched out over the pool with a particularly large and obvious grasshopper dangling on the end, and P.H. appeared on the other bank. Absolutely true to form he said not a word, but I knew he'd seen me, and he knew I knew. The next day he came again and, by superb casting, put a fly up under the thorn bush and caught a good trout. It was the perfect squash, and I've seldom felt so small.

All the same, I would strongly recommend dapping with the grasshopper as a prime stimulant of adrenalin, where it's allowed, of course.

To be realistic, the bending, or indeed shattering of fishery rules is by no means confined to war-time or to the young. Just as most honest drivers would agree that they seldom complete a day's journey without committing some motoring offence, however minor, most fishermen would probably admit to an occasional lapse in moments of stress or extreme deprivation. I had only been a member of the Piscatorial Society for a couple of years when I appeared quietly and unexpectedly at the end of the footbridge over the Lambourn, which leads to the lake at Donnington. On the lake, with its rainbows, both wet and dry fly were allowed but on the Lambourn it was dry fly and Skues-type nymph only. Standing on the bridge was one of the oldest and most distinguished members of the society, dangling something into the fast water below the bridge. When he lifted it momentarily from the water I thought it was an actual worm, but it turned out to be simply a large Worm Fly – equally heinous in the circumstances.

Matthew was with me. He was then aged about thirteen and far more of a purist than I shall ever be; it just wasn't possible to pass by and say nothing, which, rather cravenly, I would have been glad enough to do in view of the extreme seniority of the offender.

"I thought it was supposed to be dry fly only," I blurted out.

It is part of life's general unfairness that in such a case, the offender is somehow no more embarrassed than he who quite justifiably takes him to task. So it was now, and in addition, the shock of our sudden arrival caused the old fellow to give such a violent start that we feared for a moment that we might have a heart-case on our hands. He muttered something about grayling and went on his way looking completely stricken, and leaving me feeling a perfect swine.

Father brazenly admitted to me once that fishing the Coln on the water of the Bull Hotel at Fairford in Gloucestershire, he once had such a frustrating day that as he went back to the hotel in the evening he took off his Lunn's Particular, or whatever, and mounted a good sized Silver Doctor. This he plied across a hatch pool to extract a nice fish of close on 2 lbs. As this was laid out on the dish in the hall for admiration there came the inevitable question about what he'd taken it on.

Slowly, impressively, but with a word, he extracted from his box a minute Lock's Fancy, probably about size 18, and laid it beside the head of the fish. As Father slunk off to the bar, fly-boxes were appearing everywhere and being scrutinised for something approaching this deadly successful pattern.

For several years before the war Father used to take a cricket team to play against a side raised by Sir Julian Cahn, a furniture magnate who lived on a splendid estate, Stanford Hall, near Loughborough. Sir Julian lived in very comfortable style; his house had a private theatre as well as a magnificent swimming pool. In the grounds was another pool with sea-lions and penquins. Irish wolfhounds roamed about. He was extremely generous to the local hunt, and had two lakes, one stocked with brown trout, and the other with rainbows. But his supreme love, above all else, was cricket, and a delightful small but splendidly-kept ground was another striking feature of the estate.

Sir Julian's personal cricketing ability could be described as moderate, but he was able to put together sides, including a few professionals, which were at least of good club standard and could probably have taken on most of the Minor Counties teams. His love of the game was such that he was perfectly happy to stand about in the outfield most of the day, and bat at No. 10 or No. 11. Occasionally he would allow himself a decorous couple of overs of bowling.

When Father's team went up for a two-day match, the entire team was lodged in the Black Boy hotel at Nottingham at Sir Julian's expense. Out at the ground there was a marquee, and at intervals during the match delicious meals were served. It all now seems like something from another world, which in a sense it was.

The fishing was tremendous, as indicated by this diary entry:

June 5th 1937

> *"To Sir Julian Cahn's – had a wonderful time., Landed 25 trout from ¾ to 2¼ lbs . . . On one occasion I had two on at once and a third fish was trying to take the top fly"*

It was in the summer of 1939 that I was for the first, and as it proved, only, time, allowed to accompany the team, not to play, but armed with permission to fish the lakes. The only stipulation (by Father) was that I must turn up in the morning to greet our host, and also appear at the tea interval.

The lakes were very well stocked and not so very often fished. On the other hand, casting was not easy; I had by that time attained a fair standard of proficiency, but in many of the most productive places the banks were well wooded. The technique of the side-cast had to be very rapidly developed, and even the catapult-cast was pressed into use at one point.

Two fish in particular stick in my mind, both browns. At one particularly wooded corner it was possible to look down into a clear hole among the weed. It had a clean sandy bottom; visibility was excellent, but only at that point. As soon as a fish moved off the sand, it vanished from sight. What amounted to a shoal of fish patrolled the area, keeping steadily on the move. There were about seven or eight trout ranging from about 1½ lbs. to a possible 4 lbs. The problem was that because of the trees it was only possible to fish from immediately above the hole, and on the first attempt the fish bolted as soon as I moved the rod.

As soon as they'd gone I cast out again, and let the fly sink to the bottom. Ten minutes later, they appeared again over the sand. Without moving the rod I drew in the line by hand; as the fly moved up through the shoal it was immediately seized, needless to say by the smallest trout on offer. It was a highly satisfactory operation, all the same.

The other fish, which weighed about 2 lbs., was also under the trees, but cruising a route quite well out from the bank. Nothing approaching an overhead cast was possible; my best effort was an inexpert side-cast with convulsive lurch at the end in an effort to get the fly out and away from the bank. It landed at least six feet away from the fish, and none too lightly. "Blimey, mister! What a whop!" was the comment Father alleged he'd had made to him on some similar occasion. In that clear and still (because sheltered) water, six feet was plenty good enough. The trout turned immediately and just charged the fly, taking me so much by surprise that I was too slow to snatch it away and hooked him well.

Fishing under trees has always struck me as very good value. On the lake at Donnington one day, right at the bottom end where it narrows to rejoin the Lambourn via a sluice, I once found a trout carrying out an almost stylised circular cruising route. He was visible practically the whole way round. Lying in wait in the lea of a tree I watched him come into range, then managed to slam the fly down far too hard and right on his head. There was an angry boil, and he disappeared. Standing there cursing myself I realised too late that the leader was sliding away; he had come back for the fly, but I missed him. It occurred to me afterwards that he was probably quite used to various prey falling in quite violently, and that his first dash away was just an instinctive reaction from which he'd immediately recovered.

Matthew tied up an extremely effective beetle-ish fly for this under-the-trees work, and if you could manage to get it to the trout in the hairy places under the trees, they took it with great confidence.

At Stanford Hall, the tedium of having to break off fishing and go back up to the marquee for tea was relieved on the first day by an attack on the person of Sir Julian. It was a hot day, and plenty of wasps had turned up to enjoy the spread. Sir Julian resolved to deal with this, and was stalking them one by one with a jammy knife when a particularly determined specimen zoomed up his trouser leg and stung him painfully on the calf. I was unable to resist a snort of laughter which, though swiftly stifled, earned me a sharp clip round the side of the head from Father.

The visit only allowed one late evening's fishing and of course I stuck it out until it was well dark. At this point Father appeared to see how I'd got on and to escort me back to the house. We walked up the hill through the warm darkness, and as we neared the buildings we were startled and, at least in my case, terrified, by a sudden clamour of barking. Visions of being torn to shreds by the Irish wolfhounds fortunately faded as we realized that in fact we were just passing the sealion pool. Father reckoned he'd known that all along.

Another friend from High Wycombe was Percy Goodearl, a furniture manufacturer, and, later, a tenant of the West Wycombe fishing. There were in those days far fewer car-owners, but P.G. had what was called (I think) a Ford Vee Eight, which he drove with considerable elan. The road from High Wycombe to Marlow was first very much widened and straightened after the war, and subsequently replaced altogether by a dual carriageway. But in those days a swift turn along that winding road with P.G. at the wheel was enough to bring a certain pallor to the cheek of even the most stout-hearted. Inadvertently, I did manage to slow him up on one occasion. We were off down to Romsey, P.G. and Father in front and me in the back. I had recently acquired a Jew's Harp, and was busy trying to get some sort of a tune out of what must surely be the most tuneless instrument known to man. After a while P.G. stopped the car, walked all round, peered underneath, and eventually resumed the journey at a markedly slower pace. At the next stop, the bonnet came up. Eventually he was going so slowly and quietly that the source was revealed of the noise that had caused such concern. The Jew's Harp was banned for the rest of the journey.

Undoubtedly Father's activities on the cricket and football fields were largely responsible for making him well-known to, if not necessarily bosom pals with, quite a large cross-section of the people of High Wycombe. It was then quite a small place with a population of perhaps 25,000, a great many of whom would have seen him play at one time or another. Other eccentricities also drew a certain amount of attention. On one occasion he was setting off early to shoot, and the car stopped to pick up another passenger in the High Street, just outside the Red Lion. Rooks were flighting to and from the trees on Castle Hill; after a minute or two of waiting, Father's patience evaporated. When the belated passenger arrived, Father had his gun out, and dropped a quick right-and-left of rooks stone-dead in the High street before jumping back in and urging the driver on his way.

In the thirties being hard up was by no means an uncommon condition; indeed even the relatively well-off lived in a far more sparse way than the majority of people would now find acceptable. Despite Father's spendthrift nature, we must, I suppose, have been in what sociologists would call the 'upper quartile' of the population of the town where income is concerned. Father shot, fished and played cricket; my brother and I went away to school, and we fed pretty well. Yet we never owned a house until about 1936, and never had a car at all. The house was not centrally heated, and we had no telephone. Despite Father's convivial nature there was seldom anything much to drink. I remember P.H. coming to lunch one day and being offered a glass of cider by my mother, since that was all that was on offer apart from water.

"No thanks," he intoned solemnly. "I never touch rattlebelly."

One name which crops up fairly regularly in the diaries is Dove, never referred to by his Christian name or even an initial although he and Father were certainly friends for years. Dove had been severely wounded in the head in the 1914-1918 war and apparently had a silver plate built into his temple. When I was about twelve he took me on my very first outing to the theatre (*White Horse Inn*) and subsequently to a meal at the Flyfishers Club. I spent most of the time trying to spot the famous silver plate which was, of course, invisible.

Probably the most consistently mentioned friend is Rupert White, who took part in fishing forays to the Thames, Misbourne and several others, but notably the Test. At first he often used to bring along his sister Marjorie, who was obviously an extremely lively girl. She drove a car with great spirit, and caught several salmon. When R.W. married, father was the best man and, rather unusually, received a present from the groom. This was a superb split-cane fly rod which I still have, although over the years a combination of hard work and neglect has reduced it to being cut down as an emergency spinning rod.

Quite appreciably harder-up even than Father was Mac Abbott. Passionately interested in all field sports, he never had the means to indulge this passion as he would have wished. When all else failed he could be found in a deckchair on the lawn of his house, reading the paper and occasionally picking a sparrow off the gutter with an air-rifle. But if Father was feeling unusually flush he could sometimes afford to take Mac down as his guest to Broadlands, where at the age of about twelve, as already recorded, I had the great pleasure of being present when he caught his first salmon.

The war gave Mac his chance. He went into the Royal Air Force, was commissioned and reached the rank of, I think, Squadron Leader and finished up somewhere in Africa, where he stayed and became what one is probably no longer allowed to call a 'white hunter'.

Chapter Twelve

On September 1st 1939 the Germans invaded Poland, and I shot my first partridge with a .410. This was above High Wycombe on a hillside now covered with houses as far as the eye can see. Father had sent me off to bring in a stubble field, and I walked right into the middle of a covey, one of which was unlucky.

On September 3rd, the whole family was gathered ceremoniously around Father's bed, where he was reading the Sunday paper; the wireless was on and we listened to Chamberlain announcing the declaration of war. Father seemed to find the news invigorating.

That Christmas we all went off to stay at the Lake Vyrnwy Hotel, largely for the shooting. The steep hills provided some unusual shots, and I don't think that since then I've ever shot a pheasant going away beneath me. On one arm of the lake the road crossed by a substantial bridge, and when a flock of duck was spotted at the end of the inlet, an operation was launched to bring them to book. Father crept into position on the bridge, peering over the parapet. The rest of us made a wide circuit and appeared behind the duck, which sprang, and headed back towards the lake. All appeared to be going according to plan, and Father braced himself to stand and take out a right and left as they swept over the bridge. Alas, they never did but simply kept going, to shoot underneath it. A quick dash over the road was rewarded only by a back view of the retreating duck about a hundred yards out.

Between the declaration of war and Christmas, my brother, who had been coasting somewhat, academically speaking, was galvanised into action. It had always been his intention to try for a regular commission in the Royal Marines, and suddenly the real incentive was there. He worked hard at a crammer's, and just before Christmas passed the necessary Civil Service Commission examination more than creditably. The Lake Vyrnwy trip was in celebration of this. Commissioned before his 18th birthday, he was off to Eastney Barracks, Portsmouth not long after Christmas. The following summer, still well under half-way through what, even in wartime, was still an eighteen-month training course, he and his fellows were going in for a very different kind of shooting as every ancient artillery piece or machine-gun was pressed into use to beat off the persistent air attacks on the naval base.

After that Christmas, the family only came together again all together on perhaps four or five occasions over the next five years, although one or two of us might be able to meet separately. The house was sold. Father, as already related, managed to get back into the army. My mother, although almost forty, to the intense astonishment of the family got herself into the Auxiliary Territorial Service (now the Women's Royal Army Corps). She too had gallant visions, perhaps of manning the anti-aircraft guns, but instead was roped in for catering, eventually becoming commissioned and finishing the war as the first ever woman catering officer of the Royal Engineers depot at Chatham. When she joined up, however, almost her first job, along with other recruits of mature years, was to patrol the grounds of the ATS quarters at Aldermarston, armed with hockey-stick, to discourage excessive fraternisation (if that's the word) between the girls and the invaders – the Americans flying in to the Berkshire airbases.

Thus all three senior members of the family were in uniform by early 1940. The house was closed down and sold. I carried on at school, staying with grandparents during the holidays.

Father's job was the procurement of arms of all kinds. In the course of this, after Dunkirk, he inevitably became aware of just how little we had to defend ourselves with should the Germans manage to get across the Channel. Most of the rest of us were fortunately in blissful ignorance, but it brought him close to a nervous breakdown.

Tensions were relieved by the great generosity of many proprietors of fishing during wartime; as he travelled about the country he was offered quite a bit of fishing, with outings at various times on the Tay, Test, Welsh Dee, Wye in Herefordshire, Liddle, and also on those delightful Derbyshire streams, the Wye and Derwent, around Bakewell. Here I joined him for a few days of convalescence, having been blinded in the left eye by a catapult shot from one of my friends during a dormitory skirmish at school.

Had this happened thirty years later Father would no doubt have sued the school, the other boy's father and anyone else in sight, and gone off with a sackful of money. In those days it was just tough luck, although I believe he did have a try. There was no National Health Service, and the surgical and medical bills must have been a real blow to his always shaky finances.

In August of 1940 Father was living in a house in North London, somewhere near Barnet, which had been lent to him complete with butler and housekeeper, by Rupert White. RW was somewhere else, but the house was kept in full running order by Mr and Mrs (unbelievably) Trout.

I suppose many fathers would consider a London house in the

height of the blitz a most unsuitable place for the convalescence of an injured fifteen-year-old boy. No such thought entered Father's head, and indeed most of the action took place well south of us at that time. We were entertained nightly by searchlights and the sound of bombs and gunfire, but never seriously incommoded.

Father left for his office each morning, leaving me to be fussed over and thoroughly spoiled by Trout and Mrs Trout. Delicious meals appeared at regular intervals, and in between whiles I would be tucked up in a deck chair on the verandah with plenty of rugs and books. On a chair beside mine was a heavy air pistol with which I used to let drive at the rats which were bold and numerous at the time, quite prepared to be on the move in daylight. It was an extremely agreeable existence.

In the evening, dinner would be ceremoniously served. I had never before (and have never since) been exposed to quite the calibre of domestic service administered by the Trouts, but could very soon get used to it. Trout, apart from being first-rate at his job, was also a man of wide travel and experience. He unbent sufficiently on one occasion to give me a graphic rendering of an African war dance he had once witnessed – it had an effect all its own when executed by a substantial figure in black jacket and striped trousers.

In 1941, Father managed to organise a brief stay at the Rutland Arms in Bakewell, and we took a great many trout, though rather small, and a few grayling. The most painful episode was one day when it became necessary to make a change of fly. Father's sight was going a bit, by this time, but he still had not got round to wearing glasses. For my part, the surviving eye had not yet fully adjusted to doing the job on its own, and a rather keen eye-watering wind did not help. We got the fly off all right, but then found that neither of us could see to get the gut through the eye of the small dry fly which was to take its place. The trout continued rising busily, the exasperation level rose to an unbearable pitch; harsh words were exchanged, and eventually we had to walk back to the road and enlist the help of a bemused passer-by. That night Father appeared in the bar with a powerful monocle, picked up in a junk-shop, but mercifully he never got into the habit of wearing it.

I only once fished in Derbyshire after that, staying with a friend at the Izaak Walton Hotel on the Dove, another lovely limestone stream. He had been there a few days before my arrival at about tea-time one day. Having booked in to a deserted hotel, everybody else being on the water, I strolled down for a cast or two before dinner. On the far side of the very first pool, a fish of about a pound was in position. I covered him, and he tipped back to drift back about a yard, apparently balancing the fly on his nose, before eventually sucking it in. This seemed a fair start; back at the hotel I put him on the tray provided and went up to change.

There were some curious and not altogether charitable glances when I joined Hugh in the bar. Apparently not a fish had been caught for the previous two days, and my methods were under some suspicion. They needn't have worried. I fished for the next two days and never touched another fish.

The war dragged on, and only about three weeks before the end, Barry was killed in action. After finishing his training he had been posted to the battleship Barham, which was sunk before he got there. He then had a period in the battleship Queen Elizabeth, stationary in Alexandria harbour since some Italian frogmen punched a hole in her bottom and dropped her on to the sea-bed, fortunately only a matter of a few feet. Drills and training went on as usual in the doubtless vain effort to persuade any passing spy that nothing had happened.

There followed a period of extremely active service in the light cruiser Penelope, running convoys to Malta. Then it was time to move into 46 R.M. Commando, which went into France on D plus about 12 hours. With a break of a few weeks he went right through and into Germany, according to the BBC commentary at the time being the first man across the Rhine at Wesel. Then, while the papers at home were beginning to assume that it was all but over, his troop ran into very heavy opposition in woodland near Hademstorf. Barry, his Troop Sergeant Major, and one of his subalterns were killed, the other subaltern wounded.

Barry's death altogether knocked the stuffing out of Father for the best part of the next year. We both happened to be in London on V.E. night when victory over Germany was announced, and joined the vast crowd which gathered outside Buckingham Palace to cheer, shout and sing. For us it was a hollow celebration.

Father's younger brother Stanley had been killed in the trenches during the first world war. Indeed it is said that he himself saw the body carried from the trenches. He found it impossible simply to accept this second blow. Through correspondence with surviving members of 46 R.M. Commando he built up a picture of the action that ended in Barry's death. Eventually he even managed to get himself across the Channel, and spent days walking the ground where it had taken place. Inevitably, he managed to convince himself that if the battle had been fought differently, all would have been well. It was all quite pointless and unproductive, causing a good deal of distress to the rest of the family as well as himself.

On May 25th 1945, a few week's after Barry's death, Father took himself off to Romsey for a week's fishing. I imagine that word of his loss had got round among the people there, for he had invitations to fish several waters, including those of Broadlands House itself. I came to join him for a day or two, and with Father, met General Sir Alan Brooke beside the river. He also must have had some fairly sombre memories to temper the satisfaction of victory.

Although the holiday was inevitably blighted by his bereavement, Father got several good fish during the week. Broadlands Park yielded two trout at 2½ lbs. and 3 lbs., both on Barratt's Spent Gnat. He was also broken by 'an enormous fish, about 10 lbs'. The diary does not reveal whether this also was on mayfly, or whether he too had been allowed to try 'a local lure'. The Memorial Park produced a fish of 2¼ lbs., but Testcombe and Nursling did nothing very much.

Shortly after the war finally came to an end with the defeat of Japan, I found myself serving in Palestine with 6th Airborne Division. Although my possession of only one good eye had put a regular career with the Royal Marines out of the question, it had proved not too difficult to circumvent the medical man to whom I presented myself for enlistment in the army. To this day I can recite by heart the bottom line of the sight card then in use.

By way of distraction Father had wangled himself off the staff and into the Pioneer Corps, with a posting to the Suez Canal Zone. I went down on the railway through Sinai to visit him in his fairly dreary mess somewhere in the neighbourhood of Tel-el-Kebir, a noted supplies depot where the thieving (not necessarily by the local inhabitants) was on a gigantic scale; it was related that an entire field laundry had disappeared one night.

When I got there, Father had already managed to fall over a rockery in the dark, and broken his arm. His posting home was in the pipeline, but the outing to foreign parts had cheered him up. We were not able to organise any fishing, but did see a most ingenious local method of catching mullet. The shoal would be slowly surrounded by a net, hanging down from floats and probably not more than about six feet deep; certainly it came nowhere near down to the bottom of the lagoon off the Sweetwater Canal where all this was taking place. Attached to the top rope was a further piece of net, which this time lay almost flat on the surface, stretched out on canes and supported at the outside by further floats. When the net had been drawn into a circle, completely enclosing the fish, they could easily have escaped by going deep. No doubt some did so, but a great many, having circled the netting, went for freedom over the top. Even the finest hurdlers could not manage the necessary six feet, and as they flopped into the flat net, the fishermen paddled round the outside scooping them out.

I was due for demobilisation in about August 1947, and both the parents decided to go back to civilian life at the same time. The problem was how, since by that time the house and most of their other worldly goods had long since been disposed of and all three of us had more or less what we stood up in, plus our 'post-war gratuities,' amounting in my case to about £80. I was due to go up to Oxford in October, but for them the only solution was to find some job which, like the army, provided accommodation.

By the summer they were installed at Poundon Hall, in north Buckinghamshire. At least, they were installed in three rooms of it; the rest of the house was packed with 'displaced persons' or, as they were officially entitled, European Volunteer Workers. They were predominantly Ukrainian, but also included Latvians, Hungarians and other nationalites. Most had suffered appalling privation, and had been battered about endlessly between the Russians and the Germans. At least one had been a sergeant-major in the armies of both sides. He was regarded as a highly dangerous individual, and indeed was shortly hauled off back to Germany for questioning. Unofficially, and probably illegally, Father arranged for me to be his escort to make sure he got on the boat. I spent a nervous time on the journey expecting to be pushed under a train at any minute. He spoke practically no English, and we had a virtually silent journey until it was time for us to part company. His face then broke into a broad grin; he stuck out his hand and said,

"So long – keep smilin'!"

Clearly a born survivor.

Among the EVW's were two Latvians, Fred and Ingrid Goetz, a splendid married couple who did most of the cooking. They struck up what proved to be a lifelong friendship with my parents, and moved round with them to several other camps up to the time Father died in 1953. Like others at Poundon they had a genius, borne of long practice, for making themselves as comfortable as circumstances would permit. Any room they found themselves pitched into very soon looked like home.

Tremendous celebrations were laid on for Christmas 1947. The residents of Poundon Hall were divided into several groups, indeed factions, which regrettably were not always in harmony. Although they fed communally, they had what amounted to different messes where each lot carried on its own form of junketing.

It appeared that pike was a highly-prized Central European dish at Christmas, and Father and I were sent off to a nearby lake to try for one. Not much of our tackle remained, but the split-cane salmon rod and Nottingham reel were still about, and we found a few spoons.

There was a boat on the lake, but it had not seen much in the way of maintenance during the war years, and took in a fair amount of water. The weather was extremely cold. As tears coursed down the cheeks, and dew-drops gathered at the nose ends, we drifted about the lake, Father doing most of the spinning, while I did most of the bailing. After about two hours he finally hooked a fair fish, which let go just as he got it close to the boat. We beat a retreat, and told Fred he'd have to manage without.

Despite all the post-war shortages and difficulties, the Poundonians had assembled a formidable stock of drinks for that Christmas. Father and I were called upon to make a tour of all the 'messes', taking a drink or two at each. No token sipping was accepted. We were fortunately spared the methylated spirits which a number of the hardier sorts were certainly drinking. (I always liked their dainty habit of mixing in a little orange squash) I did not manage to avoid at least one slug of something which they manufactured by tapping the sap of birch trees. We managed honourably to complete the tour, and fell gratefully into bed.

More than thirty years later I finally got round to delivering a pike to Fred and Ingrid. This came from the Piscatorial Society's excellent mixed fishery on the Kennet at Chamberhouse, near Thatcham, now relinquished. When the trout season finished we were encouraged to get out our spoons or dead baits and set about reducing the pike population. It seems reasonable to suppose that this reduced the losses of trout, but it would be hard to say so for sure. But the pike-fishing was good fun in its own right. My favourite method was to use a wobbled sprat; this is not as energetic as spinning with an artificial, and allows much more slow and thorough searching of the slack corners where the fish generally lie. At lunch-time, you can leave the sprat lying on the bottom with every chance that a pike will shovel it up (or indeed a trout, as you have heard).

Chamberhouse proved an excellent place for introducing my own sons to fishing. The pike, though a tough nut, is blessedly un-fastidious, quite prepared to take a sprat however presented, fast, slow or stationary, right-way up or upside down. Clearly a really good and thoughtful presentation, varied to suit the particular lie, will in the long run take more fish, but the boys' early efforts were quite good enough to ensure that they all caught pike. For the instruction and encouragement of boys, pike have another great virtue, in that something which is quite small judged as a pike seems quite hefty when regarded simply as a fish.

On the day Edward, then about eight, caught his first, we had seen a mink hanging about around the iron bridge at the bottom of Chamberhouse. We'd forgotten all about this when we lovingly stowed the fish away in the rushes to be collected later and taken home for admiration and fish-cakes. Eventually the mink returned, and when we went back for the pike, it was gone. Edward got quite savage.

A further fishing opportunity presented itself during the Poundon days. Not far from the village of Cottisford in north Oxfordshire someone had cleared out a small lake and stocked it with trout, both brown and rainbows. Father was given permission to fish, and we went over by taxi. The diary records that we killed seven trout up to 2 lbs., and returned nine – all were taken on Alexandra (shades of Bateman!). My main memory, however is of the sudden appearance of the vee made by a swimming snake. Father, whose sight was even worse by then, saw the movement without identifying what it was, and immediately covered it. By sheer ill luck he hooked it. Clearly since I was at this point ghillie it fell to me to net and unhook the wretched thing; fortunately the hook was barely nicked into a scale and came away with no damage. My main concern was to hope Father was right in his insistence that it was a grass snake and not an adder. It was, of course, but I notice he kept well up to his end of the boat.

Amos, the taxi-driver arrived early to watch for a while. While he was there we hooked a couple of extremely aerobatic rainbows. The effect on Amos was remarkable. Excitement would have been understandable, interest only to be expected, disapproval always a possibility. In fact he simply became convulsed with laughter, and every time the trout jumped, fresh peals echoed over the lake. It seemed a strange reaction. If we met him in the pub weeks later we only had to mention the matter and he would be off again.

The establishment at Poundon was eventually closed as the people completed their probationary period and were allowed to go off and find regular jobs. This was fairly easy for those with manual skills, but rather tough for professional people such as lawyers, whose expertise was none too relevant to British conditions.

It was about this time that Father caught his very last salmon at Broadlands.

April 20th 1948

> *"No. 1 Beat with Claud. Several fish about . . . I got a nice 12 lbs. fish on a prawn and float in Long Reach . . . river not the same since the Catchment Boar messed it up."*

Father and Mother, with Ingrid and Fred Goetz, moved on to the discouragingly named Starveall camp near Woodstock. This was a 'Lend a hand on the land' establishment where all kinds of people came to do exactly that. The idea was to get a break from your own job, a breath of country air, all with board and lodging provided and a limited amount of pay. It was all fairly spartan, both for staff and guests. A worse snag was that there seemed not to be a great deal of available work. Father had numerous battles with the 'War Ag' (War Agricultural Executive Committee) who were supposed to be organising the work, but also went himself to see the Duke of Marlborough's keeper. As soon as the shooting season started at least some of the volunteers got work as beaters. I went along myself on one occasion and was struck by the fact that while the guns knocked down the high driven birds in great style, they were all at sea with scuttling bunnies and low pheasants on the one occasion when they were asked to do a short stretch of walking up in thin scrub.

The next move was to a similar sort of camp at Cogges Hill, on the outskirts of Witney. Here the Windrush runs through the town. By nature it is a mixed fishery; in places, heroic efforts have produced a fair trout fishery blessed with a Mayfly hatch. But left to itself the lower Windrush, at least, for the most part produces excellent coarse fish, notably chub.

Father regularly used to walk by a footpath down into the valley, over the river by a footbridge, and up the other side into the town for a drink at the Woolsack. Coming out from Oxford for visits I often used to accompany him, and one day noted that just below the footbridge, under an overhanging willow, there was a shoal of chub including a few good ones. They seemed a worthy target, the problem being the defences offered by the overhanging willow branches. A lengthy period of watching revealed, however, that

185

every now and again, one of the chub would take a turn out from the shelter of the branches, ambling downstream a few yards making its way gently back to cover. Next time, I took down a fly-rod armed with a stout leader and a large fat Alder on the end.

After he'd watched me creep into position below the shoal, Father walked on up to the pub, saying he'd be back in an hour to check progress. The season had just opened. It was a hot June day, and the flies gave me a hard time. For a long time the shoal stayed firmly under the tree; then one appeared briefly in the clear, but changed its mind and went back before I could cover it. I glanced towards the path, to see Father just coming into sight. At that moment one of the better fish of the shoal finally did the decent thing, and set off downstream. As he headed for me I stayed dead still, then, when he'd turned back towards the willow, put out the fly. It is often recommended that in such a case the fly should be put down heavily behind the fish so that it whips round to take it on impulse. By accident rather than design this is exactly what happened. The chub made one dash for home, but was soon in the net. I straightened stiffened knee joints and staggered up the bank to show him to Father before putting him back.

"Well done!" said Father giving the chub a firm crack on the skull. Apparently when he'd remarked in the pub that I was on the river trying to catch chub on the fly, he had been greeted with scepticism verging on derision. Family loyalty was always a very strong point, and he had promptly bet the principal sceptic a pint that I would succeed. He set off back to collect his winnings, dangling the chub in the landing-net. It was nice to have helped him win the bet, but a bit tough on the chub. He wasn't wasted, though. In those days any protein was welcome, if only to be boiled up for chicken food.

During my last summer term at Oxford, Father twice arranged fishing for me and a friend on two of the best stretches of chalk-stream fishing in Hampshire. This was supposed to be a necessary relaxation from the intense preparations for our final examinations.

The first outing was to the Dun, a tributary of the Test which runs through West Dean and Lockerley and falls in below Mottisfont. My companion, Hugh Mosse, owned a powerful motor-bike. I was on the pillion, carrying all our gear and lunch in a rucksack on my back. Saddle-bags would have been the correct way to carry a load, but the bike possessed none, and I had an extremely uncomfortable journey, teetering dangerously on the pillion at every jolt.

We presented ourselves at the front door of our host's house, to find rather embarrassingly that he was not expecting us and indeed, had no idea who we were. It seemed that Father had somewhat over-reached himself, sending us down there on the strength of one of those 'You're welcome to come down and fish some time' kind of invitations, which moreover had apparently been extended a matter of years before.

Very kindly indeed, despite the gross liberty, our 'host' acted as just that, and allowed us to fish. His forgiveness even extended so far that Father and I also fished there together on another occasion. Neither day produced anything very startling, but the second was noteworthy for something which has turned me into a perhaps excessively mobile fly-fisher ever since.

On that day with Father, we were rod-sharing. Throughout the day there was very little fly, and almost no activity. We kept patrolling up and down, and eventually in a little sheltered bend, came across a localised hatch which had got quite a few fish going.

Without moving more than ten or fifteen yards we made contact with seven or eight trout, though not all were landed. I've frequently found since then, on many waters, that although there may be no general rise, in some small corner or another a few fish, perhaps only one, will be on the feed.

The other outing, on which Hugh again came along, was at Chilbolton, on the upper Test. This, fortunately, was a properly authorised affair – no red faces. The water belonged to Mrs Disraeli, widow of Coningsby Disraeli, Benjamin's nephew. He had inherited the house at Hughenden and, as far as I know, Mrs Disraeli moved down to Chilbolton after his death. The fishing consisted of a stretch of the main river, and a carrier which ran down in front of the house.

Though the situation was never spelled out, it was fairly clear in my mind at least that Hugh, the less experienced fisher and with no previous time on a chalk-stream, stood more or less *in statu-pupillari* to me. Unhappily, that is not how it turned out in practice. I had a perfectly hideous day, at one point losing a complete leader when my knot joining it to the line came apart. A good fish came unstuck, and I put down several others. The knife was well turned in the wound when I rejoined Hugh to find he had two fish on the bank.

"Where did you get them?" I asked.

"It was just about there," he said, putting the fly into a run below a weed-bed. The fly disappeared into a nice ring, and that was number three.

For 1950 and 1951, Father's diary records bleakly "No fishing – much hospital." The very last entry was on May 28th 1952, when a visit to Testcombe produced a trout of a pound on a dry Red Tag. Under "Remarks" comes the brief comment "Tail end of the mayfly; — insisted on spinning."

In that year, he and Mother went off to run yet another camp, this time at Linton in Yorkshire, where the local authority ran some kind of boarding school. The river Wharfe ran close by, with first-rate trout and grayling. But by then he was nearly out of steam. Not quite – he recounted with great glee the uproar which had resulted when, waiting at a bus stop, he idly poked with his walking-stick what he thought was a cherry, lying on the pavement. It turned out to be the red-painted big toenail of a woman in sandals.

In 1953 he died of lung cancer in the hospital at Leeds, and that was the end of fishing with my Father, at least in reality. In imagination he is still very often with me, most especially whenever I pass by Thames or Test.